The
E-Ticket
Life

The E-Ticket Life:
Stories, Essays, and Lessons Learned from My Decidedly Disney Travels

Kyle Burbank

Foreword by **Aaron Wallace**

Illustrations by **Ashley O'Neill**

Table of Contents:

Foreword

There are three kinds of people: those who don't visit Disney theme parks, those who occasionally do, and then there's us. We're the fans. The *crazy* fans. The ones who vacation from one Disney resort by visiting another on the other coast. We take about as many trips to Magic Kingdom, say, as other people take to the neighborhood supermarket or mall, and yet the idea of frequenting a Disney park somehow strikes the minds of many as incredibly odd. We realize, though, that there's more to savor in a Disneyland or an Epcot than a thrill ride and an ice cream bar.

These places are cultural artifacts and living works of art. They foster fun and compel camaraderie. Theirs is a satisfying blend of the nostalgic and the new. They make memories more than magic, but somehow those two things feel like one and the same in the midst of sensory overload. Figuring out why that works so well is one of the major endeavors in my book, *The Thinking Fan's Guide to Walt Disney World: Magic Kingdom*, which argues that these parks and their attractions ought to be celebrated and studied as the cultural texts and artworks that they are.

Surely "The Happiest Place on Earth" is as worthwhile as a weekly walk through the local park. And so we go and go again, twirling in teacups, grinning at ghosts, and eating more churros than anyone's doctor would sign off on. Some of us even travel the world.

I first encountered Kyle Burbank as a listener to my podcast, *Zip-A-Dee-Doo-Pod*, which has aspired to look at all things Disney through thoughtful eyes for more than a decade now. In chatting with him, it became clear that here was someone with not only a genuine passion for Disney as entertainment-art but also a truly unique perspective on the Mouse House. That's something I appreciate, hard to come by as it is, and so a friendship was formed.

I've had the good fortune to spend some considerable time in the parks with Kyle, and I'm immensely excited that others will now have an opportunity to do the same by way of this wonderful book he's written.

As it happens, Kyle is a writer both by trade and at heart. His background is in comedy and entertainment, but he also has a real poignant streak. His clever writing voice reflects that, making these stories a pleasure to read. Those who know him from his work on the popular *Disneyland Gazette* podcast, his columns at LaughingPlace.com, or his appearances in countless TV series and major motion pictures (*Big Bang Theory*, *Glee*, *Super 8*, the list goes on) will find that as no surprise.

His adventures are uniquely his own, and yet anyone who's made a meaningful memory in a Disney park will relate intimately. Kyle has a real gift for highlighting the take-away from a tale with poignancy. The essays here are hilarious, touching, and often unforgettable — whether as mundane as watching fireworks in a tree house or as epic as meeting the love of his life *because* of his love for Disney. As a matter of fact, I was there in that tree house *and* I introduced him to his wife!

By the bye, I'm honored to turn up in a few of these stories myself. Some of them even inspired my own ruminations in *The Thinking Fan's Guide*, like the time Kyle decided to tape Sorcerers of the Magic Kingdom spell cards to the end of his Wizarding World of Harry Potter wand "for ultimate spell-casting legitimacy." (I note that Universal Orlando has since taken its cue from Kyle, offering wands that do something similar in their own park — thank you, Mr. Burbank.) In reading *The E-Ticket Life*, the thing that really struck me is that even though I lived through some of these stories myself, it wasn't until I read Kyle's unique take on them that I realized just how rich — in retrospect — a simple 'walk in the park' can be.

Together, these memoirs from a young man's life paint a very sweet and utterly winsome portrait of the Disney legacy. Kyle's personal fondness for the company's creations have taken him all around the world (literally) and changed his life in oft-unexpected ways. Now, you get to come along for the ride. It's a real E-Ticket, believe me.

Aaron Wallace is a writer, attorney, and the host of *Zip-A-Dee-Doo-Pod*, one of the web's longest-running podcasts dedicated to discussing Disney. He is also the bestselling author of *The Thinking Fan's Guide to Walt Disney World*, and his movie and music reviews have reached an audience of millions. Find him online at @aaronspod or www.aaronwallaceonline.com.

Introduction

In the summer of 2009, I gave in to my growing Disney obsession and moved to California. It was an exciting change for me as it meant that I would now be living less than an hour away from my favorite place in the entire world: Disneyland. However, within only a few months of living there I had broken up with my girlfriend, nearly lost my job, and contemplated whether I really even cared as much about the parks as I once did. Over the course of the next five years, my life would change immensely. From that low point in 2010, I've rebounded. Today, I sit in my Los Angeles home with my wonderful wife and have a job that I love. When I look back at how this came to be, I can trace all of it back to The Walt Disney Company.

This revelation got me thinking about how I and several other Disney fans relate to a multi-national conglomerate like Disney in such an intimate way. Aside from Apple, I can't think of another corporation that could hold their own convention and receive as much fanfare as the D23

Expo receives. Furthermore, the adoration that most fans hold for the company starts at a young age.

As interested as I've been with Disney over the years, I've been equally as intrigued by the fandom the company commands. Beyond the obvious day-to-day joys the parks or films give us, what effect does Disney have on the lives of fans? In an effort to better understand this phenomenon, I humbly submit myself as a case study and have written this book towards the cause.

Some of the chapters in this book are funny and unexpected experiences I've had in the eight Disney parks I've been to worldwide. Others are essays reflecting on a topic that relates in some way to Disney. Add then some stories will tell larger stories about my life and how Disney or my love of it played a role in what unfolded.

I choose the title *The E-Ticket Life* for several reasons, not the least of which is the implication that life is exciting. And while I do love the Disney allusion in the title, it is important to remember that Disney does not make up our lives nor does it define it. Instead, it influences us; from the company we keep and places we visit to the morals we instill in our children and ourselves. Disney is not life but a way of life.

It is my hope this book will make you laugh, make you think and make you feel. Some of the things I share will be hilarious, others heartbreaking. I've chosen to share several aspects of my life in this book so that others can relate. After all, I've always found that the best way to relate to others is to truly expose yourself. This is what one of my favorite authors and influences, David Sedaris, does to such great results. I'm not saying I'm any David Sedaris, but I'd like to try.

Like most Disney rides, my stories have a beginning, middle, and an end, and there's plenty to see along the way. Perhaps the best way to describe it comes from a movie that was released the same year I was born: *Ferris Bueller's Day Off.* In that film, Ferris tells us the viewers that, "Life moves pretty fast. If you don't stop and look around once in a while, you could miss it." I tend to agree, and so without further ado, I present my E-Ticket life.

1
Disneyland calling

Like many people my age, I grew up loving Disney. Born in 1986, I came of age solidly in the "Disney Decade" of the 1990s. Before that, the first film I ever saw in theaters was a rerelease of *The Jungle Book*... or so my parents tell me. Speaking of my parents, I remember my mother frequently sporting a Disneyland: 35 Years of Magic sweatshirt and my father handing down to me a Disneyland license plate that he had gotten in 1989 featuring the boss himself: Mickey Mouse.

We had traveled to Walt Disney World several times when I lived in New Jersey and then, after moving to Arizona, we frequented Disneyland instead. When I was in high school, my dad purchased a timeshare in Newport Coast, which made Disneyland trips a near-annual event. Yet, it wasn't until I was an adult that my adoration for the parks really blossomed.

In 2006, I was working at a movie theater in Scottsdale that was neighbored by a gigantic, high-end shopping center. It was around the holidays and so many of my breaks were spent wandering the mall and waiting to be inspired by gift ideas. On this particular day, I ventured into the Disney Store hoping to find a gift for my then-girlfriend. Near the checkout counter was a rack of plastic cards. As I came in for a closer look, I realized they were actually multi-day and Annual Passport vouchers for Disneyland.

Surprisingly, the idea of an annual pass to Disneyland had never really occurred to me. I had just presumed such things would only be available to those in Southern California. After talking it over with my girlfriend (and spoiling the surprise in the process), I decided that at around $360 — less than a dollar per day, a salesman might add — the Premium was the way to go. In a classic move of gifting presents to others that were really intended for myself, I purchased two of the vouchers under the guise that we would be taking several trips together during the next twelve months.

We did end up making a couple of Disneyland runs that year, but I made much more use of my pass then she did. One afternoon, I looked at my latest work schedule and noticed that I had two consecutive days off coming up in the next week. That's when the notion that I could conceivably drive to Disneyland and back over the course of these two days hit me.

Now any sane person would probably drive to Disneyland one day, get a hotel for the night, and drive back the next day. But, if there's one thing you'll learn about me over the course of this book, it's that I can be a bit of a... George Costanza, if you will. Instead, I — in my infinite wisdom — set out to leave Arizona at 2 A.M. in order to arrive for an 8 A.M. rope drop in Disneyland Park. From there, I would stay in the parks until rush hour died down around 7 or 8 P.M. before making my way back to Phoenix.

Disclaimer: Staying up for 24 hours, including 12 hours of driving and 12 hours in a theme park, is a terrible idea. You should never do it! Thank you.

The drive there was exhilarating. As I got farther and farther out of town, I would continually question aloud if I was really doing this. Each time I'd assure myself that yes, I really was. I had loaded up hours and hours of Disney-related podcasts on my iPod for the excursion west, all which served to get me even more pumped up for my visit. In fact, it was those very podcasts that got me so excited to return to the parks in the first place.

As the sun came up I had already crossed into California, having made only one stop in Blythe for gas along the way. Shortly before the park was set to open, I pulled into the Mickey and Friends parking structure. Stepping out of the car, I was quickly reminded how long it had been since my legs had been properly stretched.

After a full day of experiencing the parks in a whole new way (read: alone), it was time for me to drive home. (I'll say it again: This is a terrible idea. You should never try it! Thank you.) Unfortunately, as it turned out, I had not quite waited out rush hour traffic entirely. As the minutes ticked by, I was moving inches instead of miles. I then began to believe that the 91 Freeway might have, in fact, been built by the devil — an inclination I feel was confirmed years later when I lived in the Inland Empire.

Once I successfully made it out of Orange County and, later, California itself, the road got darker and emptier. I can only attribute my continued existence on this planet to the lack of traffic on the 10 East that Tuesday night and the rumble strips they install on the side of the highway for just such an occasion. After waking up in a different lane, I figured it would be best to pull over for a few minutes. Eventually, I would find myself pulling over every few exits, stepping out of the car, and trying to beat myself awake. Needless to say, I made it home... but barely.

This next part is so stupid that it requires a third disclaimer: *Never do this!* Even after this event, I took at least three other similar trips with similar results — which, I've been told, is the actual definition of insanity — before I eventually learned to find $40-$50 motel rooms in Anaheim. These changes to my itineraries lead to far fewer near-death experiences.

As dumb as these trips were for me to take, they changed the way I looked at Disneyland. No longer was it a place I could only visit once a year with family, but was a place I could enjoy on my own terms. Pressure I usually felt to hit up all the E-tickets and catch every entertainment offering each day was gone, and I was free to treat the parks as just that — parks. The more I got to explore, the more detail I saw and the more detail I saw, the more my appreciation for what Disney had done soared. I grew up always loving Disney and now I started to understand why.

2
The Expert

Because I have quite an affinity for Disney, people seem to assume that I know everything about it. This is *not* the case, but it doesn't stop everyone from asking me anyway. Of course, writing a book about Disney will only help to perpetuate this misconception, since normally when one "writes the book" on something, they're considered an expert. But, I digress.

Far and away the questions I get most often are about "Hidden Mickeys." While I know where a few of them are in the parks, I've never been an avid seeker of these and just usually refer the person asking to a book on the subject instead. I also get a lot of queries about if Walt was really a racist, anti-Semitic, gender bigot and whether or not his head is actually frozen. Such questions are usually met with a rolling of my eyes and loss of respect for the person inquiring.

Another popular line of questioning tends to involve someone having a friend, a relative, a former boss, an old school mate, a pen pal, a family dentist, a fantasy football league member, a former teacher, an ex-girl-friend, an ex-boyfriend, an ex-cop with a particular set of skills, an ex-con with a heart of gold, or some other out-of-state acquaintance that is visiting California and wants to know how to get discount tickets to Disneyland. This might seem like a straightforward question to be taken at face value. However, the person asking is typically implying that I must have a ton of Cast Member friends with a plethora of disposable Main Gate passes. Unfortunately for them, I don't… well, I have Cast Member friends, but they don't have passes to hand out to just anyone. Instead I usually just steal part of the spiel from the Mickey and Friends Tram for my reply to them: "If you have more time to spend, multi-day tickets and Annual Passports are an especially great value."

In the parks, I am a bit more of service. My friends know that, if requested, going to Disneyland with me comes with a free tour, including history lessons, trivia, and a personalized dining experience. I can also point you to either the nearest or the least crowded restroom — your choice. I'm one of those people who guests often approach and ask, "Do you work here?" To which I reply, "No, but how can I help you?" I then usually point them to the nearest or least crowded restroom — their choice.

So maybe I'm not an expert on Disney history, the life of Walt Disney, or all of the aspects the company. While I know people that could write you a monstrous list of every imprint that falls under the banner of The Walt Disney Company, I am not nor have I ever claimed to be one of them. What I can tell you is about my experiences with the company and the undeletable mark they have left on my life. In my expert opinion, that's what Disney is all about.

3
Role Reversal

Is there any more magical time at the Disney Resorts than the winter holidays? Despite the large crowds that descend upon the parks during that time of year, the spirit of the season compounded with the Disney experience makes for an unbelievably moving display. So much so that my Christmastimes of late would feel incomplete without at least one visit to Disneyland or Magic Kingdom.

It wasn't always this way for me. Surprisingly, I wasn't even aware that Disney did anything special for the holidays until my father and I visited together at the beginning of 2008. In hindsight, I suppose I did see part of the Christmas Fantasy parade and It's a Small World decked out in lights during the finale of Soarin' Over California, but I was in no way prepared for the overlays that would greet me that day.

By this point, I had been visiting the parks more and more thanks to my recently purchased Annual Passport. For this particular trip, my dad decided to tag along for this run as he wouldn't be returning to work until a couple of weeks into January. I mentioned the large crowds the Disney-land Resort sees for holiday-time, but on this merry journey, my father and I were able to avoid said crowds. Instead of visiting before the New Year like most guests, we had serendipitously chosen the first week of January for our trip. Since this was back in the days when Disneyland still had an "off season," we managed to hit the sweet spot on the calendar right before the resort became "Refurbishmentland."

Our first brush with yuletide enhancements was Haunted Mansion Holiday. If you're unfamiliar, Disneyland turns their Haunted Mansion over to Jack Skellington and the cast of *The Nightmare Before Christmas* from mid-September through early January each year to celebrate both the merry and the scary holidays that fall in that timeline. The detail Jack — or, more accurately, the Imagineers — put into wrecking the halls was breathtaking. Aside from a few familiar scenes, the Mansion was nearly unrecognizable.

Haunted Mansion Holiday is undoubtedly impressive, but it doesn't ex-actly contain the same sentiment of more traditional Christmas fare. And so we marched forth, visiting our standard favorites while admiring the added wreaths and garland that adorned the park's structures. These small touches were surprisingly effective in bringing us back into the Christmas spirit at a time when most people were simply burnt out on the stuff.

As we drew closer to It's a Small World, my father began to take notice of the hundreds of lighting strands that were affixed to the ride's building. Even in the "off" position, you could tell that the famous attraction was surely going to be a thing of beauty once night fell. Before we entered the queue, my dad voiced aloud how amazing it would be if Disney's most hypnotic attraction had too been spruced up with... well, spruce and other Christmas décor.

Sure enough, as our little boat departed on the happiest cruise to ever sail, we were delighted to hear that the Animatronic children that resided in the ride had learned some carols to add to their formerly single-song repertoire. On top of that welcomed enhancement, each country seemed to decorate their area with nods to how their culture celebrated the season. For an attraction whose message may have become diluted a bit after over 50 years, the elements of the holiday overlay really help to illuminate (if you'll pardon the pun) its lessons.

Later that night, we would see the million-watt building in all its sparkling glory for ourselves. After standing in awe for a few moments, we headed towards Main Street to catch the Believe… In Holiday Magic Fireworks show that was to begin shortly. The crowds were still at near-utopian levels, so we were able to find a spot in The Hub to watch from.

The fireworks themselves were lovely, but not necessarily anything to write home about. That being said, Disney fireworks shows do have a way of tapping into your emotions with their choice of score and message. However, the real magic of Believe… comes as the exit music plays.

Following the fireworks' finale, Disney does the impossible as snow falls from the Southern California sky. If you're not expecting it, the effect can be quite convincing. This was the case for my father especially.

There's a sense amongst some folks that Disneyland Annual Passholders tend to become bitter and entitled the longer they retain their memberships. In the advent of the oh-so-clever blogosphere, this has even inspired some inappropriate nicknames for this type of park-goer. Though my passholdership was still in its infancy, I guess some of those jaded tendencies had already affected me.

In my mind, the show was over and it was time to move on to another attraction before everyone else on Main Street did. With that, I made my way through the exiting guests and over to The Opera House which, at the time, was playing The First 50 Magical Years starring Steve Martin and Donald Duck. Normally my father is the one leading the way in theme parks — darting around other families and leaving me to catch up lest he disappear into the crowd. However, on this particular night, I was the one pushing my way upstream.

When I turned around to make sure I hadn't lost the remainder of my party, I noticed that my father wasn't far behind but that his attention was elsewhere. With wonder in his eyes, his gaze was set skyward as he slowly rotated his head to take in the full panorama of what he was observing. I stopped for a moment realizing just what was happening: he was enthralled in Disney magic.

For a few moments as we stood in front of the giant Christmas Tree that finds seasonal residence in Town Square, my dad and I had switched places. Any skeptic in need of proof that Disneyland can make you feel like a kid again need not look further than us on that January evening. Eventually the snow stopped falling and we made our way into the Opera House.

The First 50 Magical Years has always had a way of choking me up. When Walt speaks over a collage of smiling faces enjoying the park that his dreams created, it takes everything I have not to shed a tear of nostalgia and pure joy. Watching the film that night, the emotion was ten-fold as I was reminded once again how magical Walt's kingdom really was.

Since that time, my dad has made it a point to visit Disneyland for the holidays whenever possible. The following year he took my now-step-mother to visit and proposed to her in nearly the same spot we stood that initial night. A couple of years later, when I was living in California, the three of us returned again to see the fireworks together. Even though the second half of the show was cancelled due to high winds, Main Street still saw snowfall that night.

By this point The First 50 Magical Years was no longer showing in the Opera House itself but in the lobby as the pre-show to Great Moments with Mr. Lincoln. We thought it would be appropriate to once again watch the comic/magician and his animated fowl friend before paying a visit to our 16th president. This time we strolled casually down the sidewalk, enjoyed the sights, and regaled my stepmother with the tale of how our new holiday tradition was born.

4
Troublemaker

A Disney addiction is one that can end up being quite pricey. In order to afford my growing number of two-day jaunts to Anaheim, I had a salaried job back at home. Though I started working at the theatre for $5.50 an hour when I was 16 years old, I was now a senior manager who wore suits everyday and got paid a relatively respectable rate for my 40 hours of weekly service (i.e. getting yelled at by customers).

As I moved up the ladder at my movie theatre job, there came a set of concessions (no pun intended... okay, I intended it) I had to make. One of these was an adherence to my company's strict fraternization policy. This policy stated that, as a manager, I would not develop any sort of friendships outside of work with any of my subordinates or supervisors. All of this was in an effort to prevent claims of favoritism or sexual harassment that can plague corporations of any type or size.

When I eventually moved to California, I did so alone. At the time I was dating a girl who I had been with for nearly four years, but had left her behind in Phoenix while I moved in with an engaged couple I found on Craigslist. When my district manager first interviewed me for the transfer position that was available, he asked me if such sacrifices would be a problem for me and if I knew how seriously the company took their policy on fraternizing (side note: if it were two woman hanging out, would it be sororicizing?). I assured him that I knew the policy well and that I would have no problem adjusting. In my defense, I didn't know that was to become a lie.

As I met the various staff members at my new location in Moreno Valley, there was one who I related to the most. Her name was Grainne; a red head with glasses, an appreciation for sarcasm, and — most importantly — some admiration for Disney, albeit minor. When it was slow, Grainne was my go-to staff member for conversation and soon our conversations experienced a change in venue and medium. Eventually, I worked up the nerve, courage or perhaps stupidity to invite her to come to Disneyland with me for one of my world famous personal tours I've spoken of.

While she liked Disney well enough, her boyfriend at the time took an opposing view. As biased as I am from being a lifelong Disney fan, he may have been biased the other way from having a less then stellar experience working at Ralph Brennan's Jazz Kitchen in Downtown Disney Anaheim (which is not owned by Disney, but affected his view nonetheless). Thus, I viewed each of our visits as a mission to bring her to my side.

On what was maybe our third trip together, we were eating monte cristos at Cafe Orleans when a jazz band appeared a few feet away and began performing a set. After a couple more bites and a few moments of watching the band, Grainne turned to me and declared, "You win — I do love Disneyland." While this was no small victory, the fact that we hadn't been caught by our gossip-hungry peers — many of whom visited the parks almost as frequently as we did — was an even more impressive feat.

These scandalous trips went on for months before the inevitable happened. One afternoon we were walking near the entrance to Pirates of the Caribbean when we heard Grainne's named called. Unlike when "Kyle" is yelled in a theme park and I turn around only to see a toddler with a bowl haircut run back towards their mother, the odds of there being another Grainne within ear shot were slim. She turned around only to see one of our coworkers. I turned around too and quickly realized the significance of this sighting. Instead of panicking or fleeing, I just acted as though nothing was wrong... which I'm sure was in no way convincing. Later I told Grainne to casually float the notion that we had just ran into each other in the parks and not actually gone there together to the coworker that had caught us. Seems like a surefire plan, right?

I'm not sure whether or not that coworker believed us (I'll take "no" if we're placing bets), but after a few more month of flagrant disregard for my company's much-touted policy, the rumors had grown too strong. It was on a Friday afternoon, a few minutes before I was to be off, that my general manager called me to her office. When I entered she asked me to shut the door and informed me that our district manager was on the phone for me. As soon as I heard this, I removed my hefty set of building keys from my pocket and placed them on her desk.

Of course he had known. In fact, he knew far more than I ever would have suspected. He seemed to know every time and place we had ever hung out and, when I didn't confess to each instance before hand, he would again remind me to be completely honest. It's not that I wasn't being honest with him; it's just that we must have hung out dozens of times at this point. How was I to remember that one time we went to a Subway in Fullerton to get cherry-vanilla Cokes?

As I suspected, I was immediately placed on suspension with my return date indefinite and my termination possible. The first place I went after learning I would conveniently have the weekend off was Disneyland — this time alone. If I wasn't allowed to talk to Grainne before, I certainly wasn't able to now, as any further contact would leave them no choice but to fire me.

I tried not to think about any of that while walking around my happy place, but of course worry would set in. Even though my pass was already paid in full at that point, I questioned whether spending the gas money to get down to Anaheim was really the best idea given my questionable employment status. Not to the mention the money spent on in-park dining and the inevitable souvenirs that could call to me from their store shelves and windows.

A week later, I got a call from my district manager. At the time, he was actually in town to temporarily run my soon-to-be-former theatre and

needed to meet with me. I arrived in my nicest suit and anxiously await-
ed whatever news he had for me. After chiding my behavior and reading
me a list of my wrong doings he had discovered by talking to several of
my coworkers, he informed me that he would not be firing me. Instead, I
would be transferring to the company's other California location, which
was actually closer to my house and in a nicer part of town. Some punish-
ment, eh?

I was honestly relieved that I didn't get fired, if for no other reason than
I didn't want my seven years with the same job to end that way. Then there
would be the embarrassment of telling my roommates followed by the un-
certainty of having to find another gig. But after learning that I would still
be employed and be able to afford my new life in California, I headed back
down to the real reason I moved out here in the first place: Disneyland.

5
Local

A common phrase you'll hear around the Disney community is "The Disney Bubble." This can be taken a couple of different ways, but it usually refers to the full emersion that occurs while at the various Disney resorts. At Walt Disney World, one could easily stay a week or more on property and spend only the thirty minutes to and from Orlando International Airport outside of the bubble. Although, with Magical Express and the two Disney shops in the terminal, that time might qualify for "bubble" status as well.

For many bloggers and other hardcore Disney fanatics, there comes a time when they decide to make this magical world their home. However, the cruel irony is that living so close to the bubble causes it to burst. This is what I experienced when I first moved to California.

On your first couple of trips to Disneyland as a newly minted So Cal resident, there's still a certain novelty to having the parks be so easily accessible to you. You enjoy the freedom of dropping in for mere hours, riding attractions on a whim, stopping by for special events, and noticing small changes you never would have realized if not for your weekly visits. Next, you start to learn the tricks of the trade: eating before or after going to the parks to save money, taking walkways the tourists don't know to take, and getting extra FastPasses by using the machines that aren't connected to the rest of the system (*cough* Roger Rabbit *cough*). Then, finally, you are fit to hold the title of Premium Annual Passholder.

I had progressed through these stages and spent at least one of my weekly days off going to the resort. This continued for months after my initial move. The first few times I went, I still made a point to hit up all my favorite attractions, see what was new in the gift shops, and then explore some of the rarely seen details of the park. But, at a certain point, it felt like something had changed for me.

There came a time where I realized I hardly ever went on rides anymore. In fact, when I'd try to think of one to accomplish before calling it a day, I would often come up empty and just leave anyway. Then there'd be occasions where I felt like I was just walking the parks aimlessly — and not in a good way.

As this restlessness continued, I began to fear that perhaps I was outgrowing my obsession. I thought maybe I had just burned myself out by going too often. On more than one visit, I remember walking back to the Mickey and Friends structure full of worry and sporting glassy eyes on the verge of tears. What was happening to me?

There's a give and take to being a Disney local. You have to accept that your visits aren't going to be as special if their frequency increases. Furthermore, like any relationship, the nature of it evolves and grows as both you and the parks consistently change.

The truth about living in the Disney bubble is that you need to step outside of it and explore the rest of the world. All too often Disney fans use the parks as their escape, only to discover reality waiting for us just on the other side of those gates. I'm not saying there's anything wrong with wanting to live near the parks and visit often; I'm just saying that you shouldn't define yourself by your fandom.

It took me a bit to figure this all out. What I learned was that it wasn't Disneyland that was bringing me down, but the rest of the world. By not confronting the issues I had in my life (i.e. work, loneliness, lack of motivation, etc.), my problems had followed me to my happy place and tainted it in the process.

For me, the solution came in the form of making Disneyland a treat again. As I mentioned, one thing that was bothering me was my job and so I realized that I needed to find something that made me as happy as Disney did. That's when I started writing again. So whether I decided to force myself to write before heading down or took my laptop (or old school legal pad) with me to Disneyland, I made sure that I was making personal strides before running away to the park.

Let's face it: the only people who get to spend all day, everyday in the parks are Cast Members. If you don't want to be one of those, chances are you're going to have to work somewhere else in order to support yourself in Anaheim or Orlando. And so my best tip for enjoying living within the Disney bubble is to create a great life for yourself outside of it.

6
Murphy's Flaw

Murphy's Law states, "Anything that can go wrong, will go wrong." This was definitely the case in 2009 when Disneyland introduced Summer Nightastic. The promotion included a new fireworks show called Magical, some changes to Disney's Electrical Parade, and a couple of smaller elements (the introduction of the TLT Dance Club and some lighting additions to Pixie Hollow). However, the center of the Summer Nightastic campaign revolved around a new dragon in the nighttime spectacular Fantasmic… and this is when Murphy's Law kicked in.

Throughout the summer, the new dragon (which is actually Maleficent in the context of the show, but I'll refer to her as a "him" for the sake of this story) suffered from various malfunctions and injuries. In fact, the dragon broke the first time Disney tried to use it, with some guests reporting that its neck had snapped. Ouch.

As June turned to July and then to August, the dragon was still a no-show. During this time, the dragon was famously replaced by the anti-climactic Maleficent-on-a-stick, which just featured her evilness perched on an elevated platform to fight her hardly-intimidated rodent foe. With the Summer Nightastic promotion set to end on August 23rd, it became apparent that the aptly dubbed Murphy dragon would not be ready in time. So it was even more shocking when, 8 days after the promotion's end, word spread that the new dragon was ready to premiere for that night's performance.

The day I moved to California was the first night of Summer Nightastic and so I had followed this drama closely throughout the summer while I adjusted to being a local and getting to visit as frequently as I wanted. Each time I would head down, I would constantly refresh Twitter to see if there were any rumors about whether or not Murphy might make an appearance in that evening's show. I'm pretty sure that I saw Fantasmic more times over the course of that summer than I had ever up until that point or have since, all so that I could be one of the first to snap a photo of the mechanical beast.

On September 1st, 2009, my friend and I were enjoying a relaxing and relatively slow day at Disneyland. When we stopped in for some food at the Golden Horseshoe late in the afternoon, I fell into my old habit of checking up on social media. This is when I started seeing multiple reports that Murphy would indeed be performing that evening. I tried my best to explain to my friend just how exciting this development was. While they didn't quite seem to have the same appreciation for the news as I did, they agreed that we should get a spot along the Rivers of America immediately.

Back in the day before Disneyland incorporated FastPass into Fantasmic viewing, this is how it was done. People would plop down on the concrete in front of the Rivers and sit for hours. Often people would hold multiple spots and so a location you thought was spacious would soon be cramped when the rest of their party arrived.

As it grew darker, every area began to fill to capacity. About 15 minutes before show time, a lady asked if there was a spot in front of me. Immediately after I told her she could squeeze in, she waved over a group of — with zero hyperbole — no fewer than 10 people that then came to occupy the spot in front us. Anything that can go wrong...

Honestly, I don't remember much about what happened after the lights around the area dimmed and the announcer proclaimed, "Welcome to Fantasmic." In those 15 or so minutes until the dragon was set to come out, I was glued to my phone ensuring that my camera was all set to capture the debut. I was also on Twitter announcing my presence at the scene to try and lure people over to my feed for impending news.

Finally, it was time. There was one moment where I, forgetting how the show went, thought that the dragon was once again absent before realizing that his cue had yet to occur. As the mist screens projected an image of the beast we would (hopefully) soon see come to life, two yellow lights pierced the top of the image.

The crowd immediately began to roar. If One Direction were a thing back then, passersby would have assumed they had just taken the stage (with Zayn, for the record). When the mist retracted, there stood Murphy in all his glory.

I snapped as many grainy cell phone images as quickly as I could before Mickey defeated the villain. Truth be told, I really only saw him through my phone screen on that first evening. Even as the light from the flame-engulfed waters illuminated my face, my pointer finger kept tapping that little, white shutter button in an effort to get the best shot I could.

Incidentally, Murphy's disappearance at the end of the show is actually the happy ending. However, I'm sure the audience wouldn't have minded if it stuck around for a bit longer just this once. As soon as Mickey's triumphant theme began to play, I was sorting through my photos and immediately started posting them to my Twitter feed.

By the time that giant green flash went off at the end of the show, my tweets had been shared dozens of times and I was steadily picking up new followers. Yes, it's kind of sad how important this was to me at the time (OK, it still is), but I relished in it all the same. For several minutes afterwards, I don't think I conversed at all with my friend except to update them on my Tweet statistics... I'm the worst.

As it turns out, Murphy actually still wasn't 100% operational on that first night. The fire-breathing effect that was supposed to kick off the flame-fest across the rivers didn't happen (though I'm not sure anyone really noticed). So *technically* the fully- functional dragon didn't premier until the day after I saw it, but...

What's interesting for me is that my appreciation of the evening has only grown since it happened. As pictures and video taken with more professional equipment surfaced in the days that followed, the element of community was really highlighted. When I watch them now, I see that the cheers from around the water were even louder then I remember. A few people even shout, "Murphy!" with a geeky giddiness that really sums up the evening.

Six years later, the Maleficent dragon (I guess we can drop the nickname now) is still an impressive display of Imagineering. Even as plenty of new and shiny things have joined the parks on both coasts, it still sits among Pirates of the Caribbean and Carsland as things East Coasters must see on their journeys west. Sometimes when the bickering of the Disney community gets me down, I go down a YouTube rabbit hole of videos from that night and can't help my smile when things finally worked out for the underdog... or underdragon... I'm the worst.

7
Different Drummer

For a spell back in 2007, The Disneyland Resort held a promotion called "Rockin' Both Parks." The features of this short-lived promo were audio overlays for Space Mountain in Disneyland and California Screamin' in Disney's California Adventure. Both were temporarily renamed with "Rockin" before their names (leaving California Screamin' with not one but *two* missing 'g's) and featured songs by the Red Hot Chili Peppers — a band so family friendly that the f-word had to be edited out of one of the songs Disney used for the attraction.

Rockin' Space Mountain showcased the Chili Peppers' cover of Stevie Wonder's "Higher Ground." Meanwhile, the even more ridiculously named Rockin' California Screamin' played "Around the World" from the band's album *Californication* (so there's the tie-in, I suppose). While this promotion was probably aimed at getting Disneyland visitors to set foot in the still poorly attended Disney's California Adventure, it also made the case that just the soundtrack of a ride could create a new and interesting experience.

The music Disney uses for their attractions, firework shows, and area background loops is carefully chosen. Because of this, Disney purists would likely be appalled if any self-respecting fan chose to listen to their iPod during a stroll through the resorts. However, I would argue that sometimes doing so creates a different and sometimes even more personal experience with the parks.

Much the same way that syncing Pink Floyd's *Dark Side of the Moon* up to *The Wizard of Oz* takes the film to a whole different level, so too does adding your own musical selections to a walk around the park... and, yes, I've done both. I've visited the Disneyland Resort enough times to know pretty much every song of every loop in every area of the park. For the most part, these loops stay the same, which means that they maintain the same emotion day after day — mostly "happy," given the nickname of the park and all. By bringing in your own soundtrack, you can explore nearly any emotion. Nostalgic, reflective, blue, anxious, celebratory; the music you select can display the park's atmosphere in a new light.

When my then-girlfriend (now wife) Rebekah was still living on the East Coast, I would visit the parks and listen to music that made me reflect on how much I missed her. While listening to these selections, I would also be taking in the sights I wanted to show her when she finally came to visit and took her first trip to Disneyland Park. At the risk of sounding corny, or — worse, still — crazy, I would explore the parks while listening to Death Cab for Cutie's "Transatlantism", WZRD's "Teleport 2 Me, Jamie", and Best Coast's "Up All Night" and imaging that I was in a music video and that she was appearing and disappearing next to me. Kid Cudi's "Pursuit of Happiness" was another favorite, as I'd often set my anxiety aside and contemplate the future I wanted for myself and for us.

As a kid, one of my favorite tapes was a Kidsongs video called *Ride the Roller Coaster*. That film, shot in Six Flags Magic Mountain, featured a group of children running around the park and singing various pop songs — many of which I had known from listening to the golden oldies radio stations. A score later, I sometimes like to pretend that I am in some sort of reboot of this video (that recast kids with grown men nearing 30, apparently) as I listen to my iPod and fight the temptation to break into full song and dance. Still, a lip-synced moment or two might slip by if I'm certain

I'm not in anyone's sight.

I know it's immature, but I admittedly think it's funny to occasionally listen to songs with profanity while in Disneyland. I would never say such words out loud with so many children around, but with the headphones firmly placed in the safety of my ears, Childish Gambino is free to entertain me with his own obscenely honest fantasies as I travel through Fantasyland. Similarly, it's fun to mash-up visuals from *Frozen* while listening to songs from *Avenue Q* or *The Book of Mormon* since all three share a composer in Robert Lopez.

On the other side of the spectrum, I do listen to some more "wholesome" music on my journeys as well. Since its release in 2014, Disney Hipster Andrew's album *Let's Move to Disney World* has become one of my favorite in-park alternate soundtracks. Being an East Coaster, the Hipster's songs mainly focus on Walt Disney World, but the playful aesthetic is fitting nonetheless. Unlike my other selections that bring a sense of reality to my surroundings, listening to Andrew's record only serves to compound the magic.

Given the inherent nostalgia that Disneyland offers and its close association with vacations of our youth, it seems only natural to think about family and growing up while visiting later in life. That's why listening to songs I associate with my father like James Taylor's "Sweet Baby James" (or, really, anything else from his catalog) only add to that trip down memory lane. In that same vein, I can't help but think of my mother when listening to The Beatles or Neil Diamond. Before moving out, she went through phases with both artists where they would play exclusively in our home for weeks on end. Although it was somewhat annoying at the time, this quirk served to enrich my appreciation for those artists in hindsight.

What's so great about the Disney Parks is that everyone experiences them in their own way and yet the experiences are tremendously consistent. The emotion and depth of theme Disney's carefully selected background loops provide are no small part of this phenomenon. However, personalizing that emotion is just as relevant a goal as the one Disney offers as a base model. It may not be for everyone, but to the Disney fan with the masterful mixtape, I say remix away.

8
Breaking

Probably once out of every three times I go to Disneyland, I feel like a complete idiot. That's because, as a reporter for The Disneyland Gazette and Laughing Place, part of my job is to cover the happenings and goings on of the park. During the slow times of year (and slow news days), this includes refurbishments. Thus it's not unusual to find me snapping photos of such mundane things as construction walls.

Every once in a while, a tourist might look at me strangely or wonder what they must be missing on the wooden plank that has been erected. Worse still are the times I need to photograph a new meet and greet character in the park. If I don't have the time or gumption to wait in line to meet them for myself, I stealthily snap a picture from afar like some sort of park paparazzi, capturing the image of whatever child happened to be in the presence of that character in the process.

These seemingly odd practices have actually grown significantly over the years. As the community expands, more and more people now "live tweet" and even broadcast streams from the parks. However, every once in a while your timing is impeccable, your luck overflowing, and smart phone reception strong enough to get a great scoop.

That is what happened to me on The Disneyland Gazette's official launch day in January of 2010. I had known the hosts of the podcast (Luke, Kenny, Lee, Shawn, and Chuck) from a previous show they did and had become friendly with them. Because of this, when they started a new site, they asked me to be their "intrepid field reporter." This really just meant that I'd tweet out my park adventures on their Twitter account instead of my own, but it was an exciting proposition nonetheless.

January is —or at least was — a notoriously slow time of year for the resort, with the winter holidays having passed and spring breaks still a couple of months away. Because of this, it is also known as refurbishment season. On top of that, the then-named Disney's California Adventure was still a construction maze as it underwent its huge makeover.

There was so much construction in DCA at the time that the walls being used in the process had been reported on ad nauseam. Any small change to the setup of these wooden walls lead to multiple tweets describing the route they now directed you in. One popular subtopic of this was sharing horror stories of the near pedestrian-versus-stroller collisions these narrow walkways lead to. Riveting stuff, really.

The trouble with covering such a detailed and ever changing place like Disneyland is that there will inevitably be a time where you ask yourself, "Is this new?" This usually leads to a tweet beginning, "Is it just me or..." Alternatively, there's also, "I might be crazy, but..."

As I started my first lap shortly after rope drop that morning, I came across a hardly-surprising set of construction walls in between the Tower of Terror and the Hyperion Theatre. What set these particular walls apart from the typical "Pardon Our Pixie Dust" variety was their advertising of the much-touted Red Car Trolley. The Red Cars were set to be a feature of the to-be-built Buena Vista Street that would serve as the new park entrance. Modeled after the Red Cars that graced the streets of Los Angeles in the 1920s (and not to be confused with the trolleys of San Francisco), they were to be the finishing touch on the Main Street-esque entryway.

In addition to having a large image of what one of the trolleys would look like (which wasn't news at this point), there was a sign announcing the stops on the Red Cars line. After asking myself if this was actually new, I decided to take a picture anyway. I tweeted out a wide photo of the whole construction area and a close up of the line sign.

As I hit send, I fully expected to get a snarky response within moments about how this wasn't news or even a note about just how long the supposedly-new signs had been there. Instead, the Gazette account began getting a steady roll of retweets, starting with random accounts and then growing to well known and established authorities in the Disney (lowercase) world. At that point, I figured the answer to my question was "yes" — they are new.

For the rest of the day, I was on a high. Whatever other minor news items I found were dwarfed by the coverage my trolley tip had gotten. When I walked back to the Mickey and Friends parking structure to charge my quickly dying phone, my editor, Luke, texted me with a link. As it turned out, the *Orange County Register* had written a story on the trolley stops and used my photo. To me, this was the equivalent of being on the cover of *Time*.

Luke decided to capitalize on the proverbial heat the Gazette was getting that day by releasing the first issue of The Disneyland Gazette Podcast. After getting my phone's battery up to a functional level, I went back to the park to celebrate. On the walk over, I fashioned an idea to promote the show and site further by launching a mini in-park contest. I tweeted that the first person to find me in the park would receive a Vinylmation of their choice — back then Vinylmations were still relatively new and had a large, rabid following. If enough time had passed and no one had found me, I'd send out another clue. Eventually, I plunked myself down on a bench not because I was tired of walking around but because my battery was already dying again.

Eventually, two excited guests approached me asking if I was from The Disneyland Gazette. When I answered affirmatively, they briefly celebrated before we all headed to the nearest shop (the now extinct P.T. Flea Market) to purchase their prize. They thanked me repeatedly as we parted ways and, as soon as we did, I checked my phone one last time to see what our retweet count was up to. It had seemingly topped out and so I decided to call it a night.

In retrospect, it all seems a bit silly. I mean — all I did was take a photo of a wall. But to Disney fans, it's not the wall itself that's exciting, but what they represent. Behind these walls isn't just a pile of dirt the park management doesn't want the public to see; instead, there's a carefully Imagineered project that will inevitably delight us in the future. When it came to the Red Car Trolley and the rest of the Disney California Adventure redo, the enhancements behind the walls were jaw dropping in scale. Other times, the improvements are small and recognized only by the biggest of park enthusiasts. In those cases, there will surely be a Disney blogger who walks by and thinks, "Is this new?"

2
Vinylmation

For people who haven't been to the Disney parks very often, the abundance of pin trading can raise some eyebrows. Similarly, the craze surrounding Disney Pins and Pin Trading is something I have never fully comprehended, although I am guilty of buying a few pins myself. In fact, I even went as far as to spend several of my early morning hours waiting in line just to purchase a Piece of History pin featuring Sleeping Beauty Castle. Aside from these few isolated incidents, pin trading never really became my "thing" (AKA "addiction"). That distinction would later be awarded to another Disney collectable: Vinylmation.

If you're not familiar, Vinylmations were (emphasis on the past tense for reasons that will become apparent) three-inch Mickey-shaped figures that were then decorated with various designs. Each set released had a different theme such as the Park Series (art inspired by Disney attractions), Urban (street art inspired designs that could really be anything), and, later, narrower themes were introduced such as *Toy Story* and The Haunted

Mansion.

My biggest problem with Vinylmations from the start was the fact that each figure came "blind boxed," meaning that there was no way to be sure of which figure you'd be buying. On top of that, there were also "chasers — rare mystery figures that weren't even on display. Each tray of Vinyls contained 24 figures: two copies of each of the normal designs but only one of the chaser (plus an extra of one of the normal to complete the case). Somewhere down the line they also added "variants" which were alternate versions of chasers that were even *more* rare, but I had punched out by then.

When Vinylmations were first introduced in the November of 2008, I didn't pay them much mind. Some of the designs were intriguing, but the number of underwhelming ones coupled with the high probability of ending up with one of them was enough to keep me away from the first run. I'm honestly not sure what changed, but, when Park Series #2 came out a few months later, I decided to roll the dice to blow the balance of a Disney gift card on a couple of figures.

The next part of my story can be summarized thusly: I bought some figures and yada yada yada I ended up with over 100. Soon my trips to Disneyland were mainly spent hopping from store to store looking to trade Vinyls. Once I went to grand openings of Disney Stores in order to get exclusive sets. Another time I bought cases of Clear Series Vinyls on sale in order to trade them off later… until they got wise and began disallowing this practice.

As fun as this was, there came I point when I realized just how much I had been spending on the figures. When I looked around my room, I no longer saw little works of art, but hundreds of dollars that I could be using for such things as… paying rent. With that in mind, the first step was to pair down my collection to about a dozen favorites that would survive the auction block. Next the "high-dollar" and "rare" pieces, such as chasers and Park Series #1 figures I had acquired, got listed on eBay as single items. After that, I posted photos of my collection on social media and directly sold some to my friends and acquaintances at whatever reasonable price they were willing to pay. All in all, I recouped a few hundred dollars from selling off my long-curated collection. Still, it was only a fraction of what I had spent to acquire the figures in the first place.

In 2015, Disney announced that Vinylmation trading would no longer be offered in the parks. This came as news to me since I was blissfully unaware that Vinylmation trading was still occurring *anywhere,* let alone in the parks. As I write this, there are still new sets of figures being released, but the general consensus is that the concept jumped the shark long ago.

A common criticism lobbed at The Walt Disney Company is that they are just as money-hungry as any other conglomerate, but that they trot out the ghost of their founder in an attempt to disguise their true motives. Fans of Disney fall somewhere on a scale ranging from "Everything is magical all of the time" to "Capitalism at its finest" when asked about this supposed contradiction. I tend to fall somewhere in the middle, believing that the company is rightfully driven by profits but that they also strive to achieve their monetary goals by offering the best possible experience no matter the medium.

That model has always been very admirable to me and I've consistently seen value in the products I've purchased from the company. To be fair, the same could be said about Vinylmations. They were well made and priced to meet the principles of supply and demand; how could I fault them for that? I've seen a lot of people spend a large portion of their savings on Disney memorabilia and have always wondered how they did it. However, I now think that I understand it perfectly: sometimes love is blind... and you need to open your eyes before you walk off a cliff. I followed Vinylmations to the edge, but, thank heaven, I never jumped.

"Under New Management"

10
For the First Time in Forever

It's hard to argue that there was ever any lack of Disney in my life. Yet, as I started to take more of an interest in the budding Disney online community, it quickly became apparent to me that there was a whole world of knowledge I was a bit rusty on — a Walt Disney World, to be exact. Sure I'd hear all about the small changes that were occurring on a weekly basis, but having no frame of reference to even understand these changes was starting to annoy me as my consumption of Disney news grew.

When I visited Walt Disney World in 2009, it was my first trip there in over a decade. At the time, I couldn't have even told you how long it had been because I only had small flashes of memories from that visit as a youngster. However, I later realized that my parents separated circa 1997 and that I had gone after Ellen's Energy Adventure opened. Thus, my Sherlockian logic (just call me "the great Mouse detective") concludes that my visit must have taken place in 1996. If that wasn't enough, I later remembered that Cinderella Castle was dressed to look like a pink birth-day cake at the time, confirming my 1996 deduction — the 25th anniversary of Walt Disney World. Watch out, Basil...

I moved to California in June of 2009, conveniently just prior to the first D23 Expo in September. If living 45 minutes away from Disneyland instead of six hours didn't send my Disney fandom into hyperdrive, the D23 Expo certainly did. At the event, I met podcasters and other Disney fans, many of whom I knew from Twitter but hadn't actually met in person. One such person was my friend, Benji, who worked at Magic Kingdom at the time.

A couple weeks after the expo, I was dead set on revisiting Walt Disney World. I've heard rumors that when most people want to plan a vacation they might talk to a travel agent, look up prices online, or start saving up money so they can afford to do everything they want. Instead I, Mr. Instant Gratification, took to Twitter to fulfill my wish.

As you can imagine, the Expo and my near-weekly trips to Disneyland had taken a toll on my finances. After researching prices for hotels and flights, I realized I would need at least a few hundred more dollars before I could afford to go. I don't even think that included park tickets, which I guess I just assumed I would have time to save up for.

My recently decided dream got carried away and so, one night, I half-jokingly asked the Twitterverse if anyone wanted to "sponsor" my trip. Amazingly, I got an offer one better: Benji said I could stay at his place in Orlando. On top of that, he would be able to "sign me in" (as we still say for some reason) to the parks each day since he had a Silver Main Gate pass. In this scenario, all I would need to purchase was a flight. Of course I verified with him a minimum of seven times that he was actually serious before thanking him profusely and searching for a flight. I decided to go only a few weeks later in October of 2009. Like I said — instant gratification.

I landed in Orlando while Benji was still at work. To kill time, I checked out the theme park stores in the terminal (Disney, Sea World and Universal), got some Chick Fil A, and found a nice chair to sit down and see how long until security started to get suspicious of me. Apparently I didn't take quite long enough to get on their radar, as Benji soon called to say he was nearing the airport.

Dressed in a green and yellow striped shirt and a purple, bat bow tie, it was obvious that he had just finished a long night at Mickey's Not So Scary Halloween Party. Unfazed by his somewhat peculiar look (complete with glitter on his face and hair), he exited his car to greet me and help me get my bag into his trunk. By the time we got back to his apartment, it was already pretty late and he had to wake up early to open Magic Kingdom the next day. He showed me to my ~~room~~ couch before retiring to bed. While I laid there thinking about how I would get to spend the next day in the Magic Kingdom seeing Cinderella Castle, the Country Bear Jamboree, and Philarharmagic among other things, I was reminded of my favorite Disney commercial that my dad and I still quote to this day: "I'm too excited to sleeeeeeep."

Shortly after falling asleep, it was time to wake up (before the sun, even) to travel with Benji to work. Since the park wasn't open yet, he dropped me off at The Polynesian Resort to get breakfast and wait for rope drop. He explained to me how to get to Magic Kingdom from the Transportation and Ticket Center (not exactly rocket science, but I was a newbie again — and one without a park ticket yet) before heading in for his shift. I headed into a deserted Captain Cook's to start my big Disney day with a ceremonial Mickey waffle. By the time I was done, the sun was just starting to show itself. Walking out near the beaches of the resort, I snapped photos of the ferryboats cruising across the water surrounded by a pink sky — a small reward for waking so early.

A bit before rope drop, I boarded the monorail at the TTC and was soon at the Magic Kingdom esplanade. As I approached the now-deceased turnstiles, I veered all the way to the left to get the attention of the security guard sitting at a booth just on the other side of the gate. Once we made eye contact, I informed him that a Cast Member had left a ticket for me. There was minor panic when he told me that he didn't have anything, but a moment later he opened the gate to let me in. The guard said that Benji had picked up the ticket but that I would have to go get it from him back in Fantasyland. He followed this up with, "You know where to find him, right?" I didn't exactly, but I assured him that I did anyway and headed through the tunnels.

As if seeing Main Street for the first time in 12 years weren't magical enough, doing so without a park ticket made me feel like I owned the place. Of course, the Disneyland Main Street I was used to and that of Magic Kingdom aren't radically different, but the size and scale of MK's were impressive. And then there was Cinderella Castle. I've always been a fan of the relatively small, quaint Sleeping Beauty Castle of Anaheim, but the class and grandeur of Florida's castle cannot be denied. Its only flaw being that, due to numerous stage shows in front of it, guests can't walk though the castle gates as often as they do on the West Coast.

Luckily for me, no show was going on at the time and I was able to walk straight through the castle and into Fantasyland. This is where the differences between Disneyland and Magic Kingdom really started to show. While Disneyland had ditched the medieval tent theme in 1983, Magic Kingdom still had that aesthetic before the "New Fantasyland" expansion.

Somewhere over by Peter Pan's (inferior) Flight, I found Benji. As it turned out, he didn't actually have my ticket and so I was sent back to the security guard who had trusted me with such status in the first place. After getting my credentials — I mean, park ticket — I headed off to enjoy a proper tour of the Magic Kingdom.

As I do nearly every time I go to Disneyland, I started with Tomorrowland. Once there I decided to give Tomorrowland Transit Authority the honor of being the first attraction I visited since my homecoming. I barely remember riding the Peoplemover in Disneyland because I was so young — only that I could see the Star Tours queue from the vehicles. I also remember that the TTA and Peoplemover always made me feel like I was on some sort of VIP tour, except that anyone willing to wait (at most) five minutes in line could gain access. After all, you get to go right through Space Mountain! How cool is that?

With my first ride down, I decided to check out another Florida exclusive and wandered into the Monsters, Inc. Laugh Floor. *Monsters, Inc.* is my favorite of the Pixar films (and ranks quite highly amongst all Disney films), so I figured I'd enjoy myself despite the mixed reviews I had heard on some Disney fan podcasts. The Laugh Floor replaced another attraction I vaguely remember experiencing in my youth: The Timekeeper. While it would have been nice to relive that, I couldn't stay mad at it for long. I don't mean to brag, but Marty Wazowski read one the jokes that I texted in during the attraction's pre-show. Clearly he had heard about my elite status for the day.

Of course I had to take a trip to see The Carousel of Progress, The Country Bear Jamboree, and The Swiss Family Robinson Tree House — all of which had left Disneyland some time ago. Meanwhile, one attraction that (at the time) was extinct in Magic Kingdom was the original version of The Enchanted Tiki Room. Instead, I had my first and thankfully only experience seeing the truly horrific Under New Management. Every bad thing I had ever heard about the show proved true and I left thanking my lucky stars that the abomination I had just witnessed never made its way west.

On my journey through that park, I started to piece together other memories from my trips as a little tike. The single-file seated Space Mountain was the first version I ever rode, as was the double-seated Splash Mountain. Before this 2009 trip I had assumed both memories had taken place in Disneyland. Clearly I didn't really remember much about either adventure, but the t-shirt I had purchased after riding Space proved that it had happened.

The park I had the most impressions from as a kid turned out to be Epcot. Although I had placed which attractions some of those memories had come from ahead of time, others remained a bit of a mystery. As I mentioned, I remembered an attraction with Ellen DeGeneres which was clearly Ellen's Energy Adventure. I also recalled a ride that reminded me of the ferry scene in *Willy Wonka and the Chocolate Factory*; this turned out to be Living with the Land.

As my bus from Magic Kingdom pulled into Epcot and Spaceship Earth grew in my sight, I almost felt choked up. To me, "the golf ball," which I (and presumably many others) called it as a kid, was an icon even greater than any of the castles. Riding the attraction for the first time in forever, memories of the infamous Rome-burning scent, the scene with the first printing press, and the now somewhat-outdated scene of children talking on the internet all came back to me... much like that one Celine Dion song.

It was then that I thought about the other Epcot attractions I loved as a kid that were no longer there. For one, I recalled my excitement to ride Body Wars, a simulator ride in the vein (pun intended) of Star Tours that took you inside the human body. During my 2009 trip, I didn't even realize that the pavilion the attraction had resided in wasn't even really open anymore and, instead, only served as the International Food and Wine Festival

Center.

Food Rocks, which replaced Kitchen Cabaret, featured various culinary treats performing parodies of pop songs. One of the first songs was by The Peach Boys performing "Good Nutrition." Seeing as The Beach Boys and their song "Good Vibrations" were childhood favorites of mine, the show had stuck with me even as all these other park memories had faded.

The World Showcase half of Epcot rang a few more bells, specifically the large temple of the Mexico Pavilion and the narrow streets of the Morocco Pavilion. As a kid, that pavilion reminded me of *Aladdin,* which I'm sure was actually part of the point. While riding Gran Fiesta Tour, I hypothesized that I had probably ridden its previous incarnation, El Rio del Tiempo. I also had faint memories of the park's fireworks show, Illuminations, though I couldn't tell you much about it.

Apparently the park I had the fewest memories of (aside from Disney's Animal Kingdom, which wasn't even open until 1998) was Disney's Hollywood Studios. Of course, when I had visited the park in 1996, it was still going by its original name: Disney-MGM Studios. Although I recalled being scared of the *Alien* section of The Great Movie Ride (some things never change), seeing the Indiana Jones Stunt Spectacular, and watching animators drawing (back in the days when the park was still a working studio), the place had grown up a lot since then. Years later as I write this, it seems it had even more growing up to do as the park has since changed drastically from that visit six years ago.

However, the thing I remember most about MGM was getting the meet the Teenage Mutant Ninja Turtles. As a kid, I was obsessed with the Ninja Turtles… much the way I'm obsessed with Disney now. Memorably, I even impressed my first grade teacher by knowing the word "palm" as I recalled Shredder telling the Turtles that he "Had them in the palm of his hand." The moral of the story: don't let anyone tell you TV is bad for you. Not too long ago, I stumbled upon some photos of me with the Turtles and their van. I also found my autograph book which Leonardo and — my personal favorite — Raphael had signed.

After my 2009 trip, it would be only a couple more years before I would visit Disney World again. Later, there was a time where it seemed like I was visiting every few months to the point where I considered myself an "Honorary Local." The Disney Parks can change a lot over the course of one year, let alone a decade. Like an old friend, it's always nice to catch up with them… but I prefer to never lose touch in the first place.

11
Yeah, But Which is Better?

In the eternal debate for Disney Park supremacy, I've always worn my Left Coast bias on my sleeve. Further up said sleeve, we Disneyland-ers keep the ultimate trump card to use when under attack from the east: Disneyland was the only park that Walt ever walked in… unless you count the surveying trips to buy the land for the Florida Project. Of course, most don't accept this attempt at dismissing the argument, and so, as Elsa would say, the storm rages on.

What's silly is that the argument of whether Disneyland or Walt Disney World is truly better is more or less moot. I have a feeling that anyone who's had the pleasure of visiting the Tokyo Disneyland Resort might agree since, if the debate is over resorts and not parks, the Japanese are the clear victors — a consolation for the 1940s, I suppose? But putting four parks up against two isn't fair to begin with and that's why I've maintained that the only proper way to compare the two domestic resorts is to put Disneyland directly against Magic Kingdom.

Any true assessment of a winner would have to be based on some sort of rubric that takes into consideration many different elements. For example, comparisons of all duplicate attractions would make a large part of the supporting data. However, even this raises a number of issues. The ride portion of Disneyland's Pirates of the Caribbean handily defeats that of Florida's, and yet Magic Kingdom's contains a superior queue experience. Which is more important?

Maybe instead of comparing the attractions that are the same, one should look at what's different. The fact that Magic Kingdom is still home to The Country Bear Jamboree, The Carousel of Progress, and the People-mover makes it the envy of nostalgic West Coasters. However, I think all of Southern California is perfectly content to never import Stitch's Great Escape. Similarly, maybe Walt Disney World fans wish they too could still ride Mr. Toad's Wild Ride like those in Anaheim can, but will thank heaven that there aren't any Disney characters present in their It's a Small World. For every Philharmagic that Florida boasts, California has an Indiana Jones Adventure to match it. Plus, the mountain range count is even now that The Seven Dwarfs Mine Train gives Magic Kingdom's Fantasyland the E-Ticket that Matterhorn brought to Disneyland in 1959.

On that note, perhaps a land-by-land breakdown is best. Both resorts have seen the introduction of "New Fantasyland" — though nearly 30 years apart from each other — so it really comes down to whether you prefer *Pinocchio* and *Alice in Wonderland* dark rides or *Little Mermaid* ones. Then there's the consideration that Disneyland's ToonTown easily had Magic Kingdom's beat until the latter got re-themed and engulfed into Florida's Fantasyland.

Tomorrowland, which has always been a challenge to each park, is another interesting case. Though the East Coast version looks fantastic, one could argue that the western version contains a better line-up of attractions. On the opposite side of the hub, the two Adventurelands could not be more different, while neither Frontierland has much to write home about (presumably by telegraph) that makes it truly stand head and shoulders above its sibling.

So maybe the real deal-breaker comes down to New Orleans Square versus Liberty Square. Both are home to The Haunted Mansion and some of the best dining each respective park has to offer, but both could practically be considered sub-lands. So should the entire debate really hinge on such small areas? That'd be like me mentioning Critter Country in this essay — it just doesn't matter.

With everything else ruled out, I guess it comes down to what is arguably the most important land in either park. The one you must see at least twice no matter what you do: Main Street USA. So do you fancy meeting President Lincoln or Mickey Mouse? Either way, you can grab a hot dog and some Starbucks, so I'm thinking this is a wash too.

By now I trust you've caught on to my point; there is no way to compare Disneyland and Magic Kingdom and declare a winner. Sure Magic Kingdom is grand and vast, but there's always something to be said about how quaint and detailed the original Magic Kingdom is out in Anaheim. Though the uninitiated might assume that all the Disney parks are one and the same, we as fans know that this couldn't be further from the truth. So, once and for all, let's agree to celebrate each park's uniqueness instead of trying to crown a champion. Besides, while Walt walked in only one of them, I believe he would have loved all of them.

12
Single Rider

My visits to Disneyland vary greatly depending on the company I'm with. If I'm going with my friend Charlotte, nighttime entertainment and all E-Tickets are a must... including the ride she refuses to call by its real name, opting instead to call it "Zip-a-dee-doo-dah." When I visit with Chris and Josh, we will be checking out any recent refurbs and, if it's May 4th, May 16, May 19, May 21, May 25, or any Lucas related date, we will definitely be visiting Star Tours... and taking a photo with the Cast Members out front. Then, if I'm with Luke, we will be meandering around looking for changes, visiting people... and not waiting more than 15 minutes for anything.

Considering how much of your Disney day is guided by your choice of company, going to a Disney Park solo can be a jarring change. Suddenly, instead of ride selections and meal breaks being a democratic process, such things are left to whim and impulse. In a society that so values individual expression in the face of any dissenting opinions, I find it surprising that more people don't explore the theme parks on their own. Does it carry the same stigma of the table-for-one or seeing a film sans date?

The first time I went to Disneyland alone was when I got my first annual pass. Believe it or not, I actually researched the topic online before I considered making my trek out to California by myself. What I found was that, while not entirely common, people did in fact visit the parks alone.

Most of what makes these solo-outings feel strange is based on perception. Not just what we think of ourselves, but what we think others are thinking about us (did you get all that?). For this reason, the rides I had the hardest time bringing myself to do alone were in Fantasyland. This meant that even my favorite attraction, Peter Pan's Flight, was off limits under my self-imposed rule. Eventually, Pan and neighboring attractions made their way onto my list of acceptable single rider attractions, although Dumbo and Casey Junior were still a no-go.

You're not a true single rider until you've been sworn in as one. How exactly does one pledge such an allegiance? When you get to the front of the queue and the Cast Member asks, "How many here?" and you are forced to reply, "One" or, "Just me," congratulations — you've made it. The first couple of times, your inflection might be a bit on the sheepish side, but have no fear. With some practice, you'll be The Wolf of Main Street in no time… if there were rides on Main Street.

Of course, being a single rider actually has a lot of benefits. I doubt most people realize that on several E-Ticket attractions utilizing the single rider line can often trump having a FastPass. Plus, the feeling of entering through the exit of Disneyland's Splash Mountain and getting to climb over the bridge that transports you to the proper side of the queue never gets old.

Maybe it does take a certain type of person to enjoy venturing to a theme park alone. I'd like to think it takes someone who's secure enough with themselves to look past the sometimes-judgmental looks. While some might think that single riders are anti-social, I'd argue that my experiences as one reflect some of my most extroverted moments.

This doesn't mean that there aren't a few hiccups in the plan. There's always sure to be that party whom, upon you taking the third seat in their Radiator Springs Racer vehicle, gives you a look that screams, "I think you're supposed to wait behind the gate." Then there's the family of five on Splash Mountain that will forever have a photo on their refrigerator of all of them plus the one weirdo in the hoodie they wish could have been airbrushed out.

Perhaps us hoodie-wearing weirdos should start a support group. But instead of bemoaning our Disney addictions, we can stand boldly and affirm each other's dedication to following no man's itinerary other than our own. For we are the few, the proud: the single riders.

13
On the Opposite Side of the World, a Villain Becomes My Friend

Seeing as I had mastered the art of traveling alone to Disneyland and spending time alone in Walt Disney World, I apparently thought the next logical step was a solo trip overseas. While most people might get their proverbial feet wet by first traveling to a foreign country a little closer to home, leave it to me to choose a trip to Tokyo, Japan. That's right — I chose to go to a county where not only do I not speak more than three phrases of the language but also one where the language isn't written in Roman-based letters, leaving me not even a fighting chance of figuring it out in context.

I should also mention that I've never been a big fan of flying. I'm not *afraid* of flying really, but I would frequently get headaches or feel nauseated on board when I was younger. So purposely subjecting myself to an 11-hour flight was also a strange move. But I suppose they do say to face your fears, right?

My desire to visit Tokyo had been growing since I was a senior in high school. One day during that year, my friend Mic and I drove up to the art-house theatre I worked at in Scottsdale, Arizona to see the Sophia Coppola film, *Lost in Translation.* The story follows a somewhat washed-up actor — played by Bill Murray — who travels to Tokyo to shoot a round of Japanese whiskey commercials. While there, he meets and becomes friends with another (much younger) American (Scarlett Johansson) who has been left alone in the hotel while her photographer husband is out working. Together, they learn to embrace the oddness of the city as well as appreciate its beauty.

While it seemed to take the two a while to warm up to Tokyo, I fell in love with it from frame one. The bright neon, the buildings stacked on top of one another, the crowded streets — this place looked like Manhattan times ten — and I already loved New York. Strange or not, I was sold.

It would be almost six years from that day at the theatre until I would get to visit Tokyo for myself. The idea went from "pipe dream" to "New Year's Resolution" in a matter of days, as my roommates and I first brought up our mutual infatuation with the prospects of Japan. My roommate at the time, Cassandra, stated what should have been the obvious "You just want to go there because of Disneyland." Ironically for me being such a big Disney fan, I already had my heart set on traveling there before I even remembered that there was also a Disney resort in Tokyo. Of course, once I did remember this detail, the deal was sealed.

The next step was to grab my laptop and see just how much a dream like this would cost to fulfill. Answer: not as much as one might think. As weeks passed, I was getting more and more serious about booking the trip. I was still working full time at a movie theatre, so I decided that the best time for me to travel would be in April, right before the big summer movie rush. Almost serendipitously, this is cherry blossom season in Japan and, as I would learn, is one of the most beautiful times to visit.

Eventually, my roommates decided they weren't in a good financial place to take that large of a trip and so I searched for another partner in crime to accompany me. When this failed, I convinced myself that I could do this on my own. I booked the trip and immediately began researching everything I wanted to do and see while there.

I didn't actually believe I was going to Japan (especially for the price I paid) until the wheels touched down at Narita Airport. From the runway I could see the Japanese writing and people driving on the left side of the road, but I still wasn't convinced. Once the plane landed, I then purchased a bus ticket into Tokyo (which is about an hour away from the airport), but it still felt more like Epcot to me than the real thing.

Upon arriving at Tokyo City Air Terminal (which connects to the Tokyo subway system), I forgot all of the research I had done and quickly found myself in over my head. I purchased my train ticket and stuck it in the turnstile in order to pass. However, as I walked down the stairs a few feet later a man tapped me on the shoulder and handed me my ticket, as I would need it to exit the station at my destination. Oops.

The directions for my hotel had informed me to take "Exit 1" at Hanzomon Station in order to get to their property. As it turned out, the name of the train line I would take to get there was the Hanzomon Line. Unlike in New York, the stations in Tokyo are named with a letter and number, corresponding to their stop along that line. For example, the Hanzomon line was "Z" and the stations were "1" through "10". Jumbling the words in my head, I then began to second-guess "Exit 1" and thought, perhaps, they meant "station 1" instead. This could not be more wrong.

I exited the train at "Z1" — Shibuya Station. I walked up the stairs with my giant suitcase, packed with two weeks worth of clothes, and into what is Tokyo's equivalent of Times Square. It was immediately apparent that I had made a mistake.

Even though I was rather certain I was in the wrong area that didn't stop me from casually looking for the hotel just to be sure. Instead, I found a Tower Records — an old favorite store of mine that had gone out of business in the states years prior. I carried my ridiculous bag in and, for a few minutes, was able to forget the stress of not being able to find my hotel and just enjoy the city instead.

I left the Tower empty-handed (save, of course, that embarrassingly large suitcase of mine) and decided it would be wise to find the train station. This proved easier said than done as I kept making right turns around the block and thinking I would soon see a big sign directing me to this gigantic subway station I had just come from. Eventually, I found an entrance (I don't quite remember how) and paid for another train ticket —

this time choosing the "all day pass" option just in case I made any more moronic mistakes.

After getting back on the train, I waited for four stops and exited at "Z5," or Hanzomon Station. There, clearly printed on the sign, were the words "Exit 1-3" and "Exit 4-5," accompanied by arrows in different directions. I cursed myself for how difficult I had made something that was so simple.

Let me put your worries to rest here and tell you that I did find my hotel that night. Following that initial misadventure, the rest of the trip went flawlessly. I mastered the train system, found more Tower Records stores, and even learned how to walk to Shibuya (which became my favorite part of the city) and find my way around there.

As I'd walk, I couldn't help but wonder if I, like Bill Murray's character, would meet anyone else like me to share my adventures with. It was also starting to set in that I hadn't really talked to anyone in over a week. My hotel had internet, so I was able to Skype home a couple of times, but the conversations I had with the people of Tokyo were short and not fully understood by either party. In fact, the only words I could muster up the confidence to say to anyone in Japanese were "arigato gozaimasu" ("thank you"), as I didn't want to seem ungrateful.

Before going on my trip, my father told me that going to a place where you don't understand the language is exciting because you have to pay attention to every detail in order to find your way back and survive. While this is certainly true to some degree, eventually I began to feel like a ghost around town. Wherever I was, there'd be signs and announcements made to get my attention, but I would tune them out since I didn't know what they were saying. Every transaction I had with a fast food or retail employee would just be me smiling and waiting for it to be over while they rambled on. In a city of 13 million, I was on my own.

After a week in Tokyo, it was time for me to venture out to the Tokyo Disneyland Resort. This required two trains, including a transfer from the subway system I had been using to a JR line train. While I had gained confidence over the past week, there was some worry about screwing this trip up as badly as I had on that first night.

If there was any doubt that Mahiyama Station was where I was to exit, there were several large signs welcoming me to Tokyo Disneyland to calm my fears. Ion top of that, the station tone (when the train pulls into the station, a short ringtone-like song plays over the speakers) played "Zip-A-Dee-Doo-Dah" and "It's A Small World." Even on the other side of the world, I was home and knew that I was safe now that I was at Disney. It was almost as though the Magic Kingdom were the American Embassy to me.

Unlike in the domestic Disney Parks, there is no single-day "Park Hopper" option in Tokyo. Instead, purchasing a four-day ticket, I was given the choice between visiting either Disneyland or Tokyo DisneySea on the first and second days (you could choose the same park both days or one day of each) and then I was free to hop for days three and four. I chose to visit Disneyland on the first day, as it seemed the only appropriate option.

I found Tokyo Disneyland to be much easier to navigate and converse in than the rest of the city. For one, their menus were also in English and the cashiers spoke the language well enough to take my order (while still having a printed menu close by, should any clarification be necessary). In fact, I found that many Cast Members at least understood English fairly well, although only a few actually spoke it. Overall, the most English I would get was the occasional, "Hello... One Coke will be 200, please."

My first day was amazing and I absolutely loved Tokyo Disneyland. From the technologically impressive attractions like Pooh's Hunny Hunt to the glass-enclosed World Bazaar that took the place of the traditional Main Street, it had lived up to all the hype I'd heard over the years. Because of this, I was just as excited, if not more so, to visit Tokyo DisneySea the next day. The park had received rave reviews, but when I had looked it up online, the flow and theme didn't quite make sense to me. This all changed the moment I saw it in person.

The park is jaw-droppingly gorgeous. Entering through a Venetian cityscape (which doubles as a real, working hotel) you soon find yourself looking across a beautifully clear bay to a giant volcano that happens to be shooting vehicles out of its side. If you're not familiar, the park is divided into different Ports of Call (hence the "sea" in DisneySea). Venturing clockwise around the bay the first area you encounter is the American Waterfront — the home of Tokyo's version of Tower of Terror.

On my second day in the park, I still hadn't quite gotten up the courage to ride the Tower just yet, so I spent my time looking around the area in depth. The courtyard in front of the Tower was currently occupied with topiaries as part of the park's promotion, "Spring Carnival." As I walked through the area, I heard a voice call out, "You there, where are you going?" I assumed this question was directed at me, as it was spoken in the Queen's English. When I turned around I saw none other than Cruella de Vil standing in front of me. Finally, my Scar Jo had come.

I answered her original question with a typical, "I don't know." In response, she began suggesting ideas of where it was I should be going... in the park, that is. Her first recommendation was Indiana Jones Adventure, to which I informed her that we had that attraction in Anaheim.

Our conversation was briefly interrupted by an infant who wanted a photo with the famous villain. When she returned to me, she asked if I had seen the Little Mermaid show, "Under the Sea" — an amazing performance that incorporated elaborate and intricate puppets with acrobatics. After I told her that I had seen the show and loved it, she snobbishly replied, "You don't have *that* in Anaheim." Touché.

In between visits from Asian children, we continued to chat even though she remained in character the entire time. For example, when I asked her if she knew of any good American food in the area, she responded, "There's a hot dog stand over there, but I prefer my dogs in coat form," or something to that effect.

It was clear from her interactions with others that she wasn't very fluent in Japanese either — or, if she was, she pretended not to be. As children from other countries approached, she'd learn a few words to repeat back to them in an effort to help facilitate the taking of their photo. Meanwhile, I would stand by laughing at jokes she made that were — well — lost in translation.

When her time ended, she retreated backstage. I took the opportunity to grab some lunch but came back 30 minutes later to see if she'd be out for another set. Sure enough, she emerged a few minutes later, going about the same business and attracting many visitors. This time I stood close enough to let her know I was there, but far enough away as to not monopolize her time.

During that second set, there was no time for us to speak and I began to feel out of place. I felt silly for how much our short interaction had meant to me. When she left again, I didn't bother to follow and try to get a good-bye of any sort out of her. Unlike the Bill Murray film, there would be no hug, no kiss, no mumbled final line. Instead, I made my way around the park feeling a little lonelier than I had felt before and wondering if I should have behaved differently.

I'm not sure what I had imagined. Did I expect to sit in the courtyard only to have a long-haired blonde tap me on the shoulder and announce, "It's me. Want to take a walk?" I could then pick her brain about her decision to move over here, where in America she lived, and what her favorite things to do outside of the park were. Maybe, after we parted, we would keep in touch online until, one day, we got to meet-up stateside.

I had traveled to Tokyo almost as an act of defiance, throwing all my fears and hang-ups aside and announcing that I didn't need anyone else. At the time, I believed that I could be alone and be fine and I was so close to proving myself right until then. Alas, the world was such a wholesome place until Cruella, Cruella de Vil.

14
An Ode to Tokyo DisneySea

Back before California Adventure opened in 2001, Disney explored a few other options for a second theme park in Southern California. First, there were rumors of Disney buying nearby Knott's Berry Farm and connecting the two via monorail. Then there were plans to build Westcot (Epcot but on the west coast, in case you didn't pick up on that) where Disney California Adventure stands today. Another rumor was for a park to be built in Long Beach with the theme "DisneySea."

Obviously the Long Beach version of DisneySea never happened, but some semblance of the concept made its way to Japan. In 2001 — the same year California Adventure opened to abysmal reviews and attendance numbers —Disney and The Oriental Land Company opened Tokyo DisneySea as the second gate at the Tokyo Disneyland Resort. Adding insult to injury for California-based Disney fans, the park is arguably the best the company has ever built.

I add "arguably" to make it sound as if there's anyway I could deny the brilliance of this park. But without nostalgia and loyalty to cloud my judgment, I know it to be true. While it may be hard to ever name a park other than the original Disneyland my all-time favorite, I have to admit that Tokyo DisneySea is ultimately better.

The beauty and detail of DisneySea cannot be overstated. Every inch of the park has something worth looking at. Yet, as well as each land works on its own, the flow of the park is perhaps even more impressive.

Instead of lands, Tokyo DisneySea is divided into seven ports of call: Mediterranean Harbor, American Waterfront, Port Discovery, Lost River Delta, Arabian Coast, Mermaid Lagoon, and Mysterious Island. Within the broad themes of these ports, several Disney properties find their way into the mix perfectly without any semblance of "shoehorning." Tower of Terror, Indiana Jones, Aladdin, and others all find a home in DisneySea (and soon too will 16 week Japanese box office champion *Frozen,* as the park expands).

As impressive as it is that DisneySea found new ways to adjust rides found in other parks to fit their theme, the attractions they created especially for the park stand out even more. From Stormrider in Port Discovery, to Sidbad's Storybook Voyage in Arabian Coast, to Journey to the Center of the Earth in Mysterious Island. The park's exclusives are among its very best attractions.

Though both DisneySea and Disney California Adventure sought to offer a more grown-up and exciting experience than their resort companions, their approaches vary wildly. California Adventure seemingly prioritized thrills over theme, as is evident in California Screamin' and the now-extinct Maliboomer. Meanwhile, Sea offers E-Tickets with complete and engaging stories attached. And while DCA has changed significantly since its faults were realized and corrected, Sea only has one major misstep to speak of: the dark tone of the then-titled Sindbad's Seven Voyages was off-putting to some and has since been masterfully redone.

Another front on which Tokyo has the rest of the world's Disney Parks beat is entertainment. In that arena, I believe Sea comes out on top as well. Not only are the shows they offer in Mediterranean Harbor (currently Fantasmic! and formerly BraiSEAmo. Legend of Mythica, and others) dazzling and awe-inspiring, but the design of the harbor allows a large number of guests to enjoy the shows comfortably.

Of all the compliments I could give DisneySea, I think the example that speaks the loudest is found in The Leonardo Challenge. Technically part of Mediterranean Habor, Leonardo's could stand as its own land. Despite the fact that the actual game is only offered in Japanese, one could easily spend hours exploring this single attraction that could almost serve as museum or science center.

One of my favorite things about Disney Parks is how content I am just to hang out and enjoy the atmosphere they provide. For that reason, Epcot ranks a strong number two for me behind the original Disneyland. But, given the chance, I believe I'd spend far more of my time in DisneySea than in any other park.

I can't help but wonder what would have come from the Long Beach version of DisneySea. As much as I'd like to think it would have been every bit as incredible as the existent one in Japan is, there's almost no chance that would have been reality. Budgets most likely would have done to that project what they ultimately did to seal DCA's fate.

I've heard it said that there are two types of Disney fans in the world: those who have experienced Tokyo DisneySea and those who have not. Those who have now hold our beloved Disney to a higher standard, having seen what they're able to produce given the right tools (pronounced: "muh-nee"). For those who haven't, I can't encourage you enough to correct that as soon as humanly possible.

15
Tower of Terrified

On one trip to Disneyland, my friends and I agreed to ride Mad Tea Party on one condition: we had to swear that none of us would cause our cup to spin using the wheel at the center of each vehicle. We then hypothesized that there was a certain age you hit that makes you no longer want to spin on a ride: around 25. However, I've actually never been a big fan of motion-intense rides. Often, I get a headache from Space Mountain and I even need a break after riding Big Thunder.

Another attraction trope I despise is being startled. I actually close my eyes during the Haunted Mansion graveyard scene, lest a skeleton pop up and taunt me with his frightening grin. Because of this, it seemed that The Tower of Terror was my biggest foe in the attraction world and had gone as far as to question why anyone in their right mind would be a fan of it in the first place.

This all changed on my first trip to Tokyo. While visiting Tokyo Disney-Sea on day two of my four day excursion, I had walked by the attraction no fewer than a dozen times contemplating riding. There were even a couple of instances where I starred watching the elevator doors open and then guests plunging before the doors shut again. Of course, this only served to psych me out more.

The Tower of Terror in Tokyo is unlike any of the other three versions that exist in Disney's Hollywood Studios in Florida, Disney California Adventure in Anaheim, and Walt Disney Studios Park in Paris. Those versions are all themed to the iconic Rod Serling television show, "The Twilight Zone" — not to be confused with the awful tween vampire novels and movies of a similar name. While the show is a classic in the United States and elsewhere (apparently France got the memo), this is not the case in Japan.

Tokyo's version of the Tower of Terror takes place in 1899 and tells the story of Harrison Hightower III, an eccentric world traveler and collector who owns the hotel. As you explore the lobby, you discover that several of Hightower's treasures were actually stolen or otherwise ill gotten from the various places he's traveled. One such relic is a tiki idol that happens to resemble a cross between a Tiki Room god and Experiment 626.

As the story goes, the idol carried a curse that would eventually spell Hightower's demise. One night, while Hightower is in the elevator of his hotel, the tiki comes to life and sends the elevator plummeting to the ground... at least that's what I understood from the Japanese-language pre-show. Following this incident, the hotel was closed immediately. Years later, it would open its doors once again, but only for tours. Those tours are what we're embarking on in as we enter the attraction.

Since the theming does not require it to look rundown and decrepit as its Twilight Zone counterparts, Tokyo's tower is gorgeous. I would also argue that the story is more compelling and interesting than that of the stateside original. Additionally, in true Japanese fashion, the effects in the ride are top-notch. One effect in particular (during the pre-show) left me so mystified that I was rendered speechless and required an extra moment to stare before venturing further into the hotel.

Prior to visiting the Hightower Hotel, the furthest I had gotten into any Tower attraction was surviving the library scene of the California Adventure version. Once we made our way upstairs to the elevator loading, I informed the Cast Member that I would be taking the stairs instead. Faced with the reality that this could very well be my last chance to ride this version of the attraction, I decided to at least give it a shot. I figured that if, for some reason, I later decided that I could handle the ride, I would despise myself for having chickened out and missed my opportunity to see this exclusive rendition. Besides, if I did get sick, I was on the other side of the world and would never see these people again.

To say I entered the hotel with some trepidation would be an understatement. My eyes darted from one side of the room to the other, patrolling for anything that would attempt to startle me. Instead, I was greeted by impressive visuals and a narrated story that could still be mostly understood by a foreigner like myself.

After making it through the lobby, we were loaded into Mr. Hightower's office. Once there, the story of that fateful night was told to us as portions of the office came to life. Following this amazing scene, any urge I had of trying to explain to the Cast Member's that I would like to exit evaporated. I had to see the rest of this ride.

When my elevator arrived, I took my seat, buckled my belt, and, of course, tugged on the yellow strap (or *kiiro* strap) as instructed. Arguably the scariest part of The Tower of Terror is not knowing when the drops will occur. Luckily, I managed to anticipate them well; the real question was whether or not I could handle them.

I don't remember the exact drop sequence, but I do know that the first drop was a short one, which I easily survived. We rose to the tippy top of the tower and then paused as the doors opened, giving us a lovely view of the park I would soon be leaving if this didn't turn out well. As we plunged — and then recovered quickly — I didn't feel sick. Instead, I found myself only able to say, "whoa."

As our elevator returned to stationary position, I wondered what I was so worried about. I felt perfectly fine and the effects were more awe-inspiring than scary. In fact, I had half a mind to turn return straight to the queue and ride once more.

Like with most Disney attractions, Tower of Terror exits into a gift shop. A decade and a half prior to this trip, I had ridden Space Mountain for the first time while on a family vacation to Walt Disney World. I was so proud of myself that I purchased a t-shirt to commemorate the occasion. The front of the shirt showed Mickey, Donald, and Goofy riding the attraction;

their mouths drawn wide open as if they were screaming bloody murder, with Goofy looking to be the bravest among them. Then, on back of the shirt (which I still have as part of a quilt my step-mother made for me), it read: "T-Minus 3: Your Hands Start Sweating. T-Minus 2: Your Heart Begins to Pound. T-Minus 1: Your Mouth Goes Dry. T Minus 0: Too Late."

Similarly, at the age of 24, I was so proud to ride an attraction that anyone over 40 inches high could ride that I felt the need to buy shirt with which to boast about my accomplishment. This shirt that I found once again featured Mickey, Donald, and Goofy as well as the tiki idol and Harrison Hightower himself. The design of the shirt resembled an old b-movie poster and, as I would later discover once returning home, glowed in the dark.

As I wear the shirt around the Disney parks today, few may even notice it. Most would assume it's from one of the Tower attractions in America. Those who take a closer look or know about the Tokyo version might comment on it in addition to those who might wonder why a Dia de los Muertos version of Stitch adorns my Twilight Zone shirt. My Disney geek friends might assume that I'm wearing it to brag about how I got to experience the Disney mecca that is Tokyo Disneyland, but I know that I'm really only secretly bragging about the time I conquered my fears and took the plunge.

16

DCA 1.0

W hile I hesitate to speak ill of Disney in anyway, it's hard not to do so when speaking of my first trip to what was then called Disney's California Adventure (the apostrophe 's' was dropped in 2010). I should preface this essay by mentioning that Disney must have agreed with many of my assessments, as they transformed the park and even rededicated it in June of 2012. However, my initial visit will always stick with me.

DCA opened in 2001 across the esplanade from Disneyland. The park was to be a more "adult" park than it's neighboring Magic Kingdom (the *original* Magic Kingdom, that is) featuring more thrilling rides, less characters, and the availability of alcohol — even including an attraction all about wine. However, most of the "thrilling" attractions that Disney included were off-the-shelf and uninspired. This was especially true in the now-beautiful Paradise Pier area.

Further complicating California Adventures issues was that, upon opening, Disney did not offer a Park Hopper option. This meant that those wishing to go to California Adventure had to pay the same amount as if they were going to Disneyland proper. Because of this, many opted out of visiting the new sub-par park in favor of visiting the mainstay across the way.

My first visit to Disney's California Adventure was in the October of 2001, when my family took a vacation to our timeshare in Newport Coast. Given that I was 16 and not nearly as plugged in to the Disney community, I was unaware of the bad reviews that plagued DCA at the time. Presumably my father didn't either, as we decided to give the new park at chance and experience the "new hotness" (to steal a phrase from *Men in Black*).

Upon entering, I remember being genuinely excited. Not because of the postcard mosaic tiles or for the promise of a new Disney experience, but because The Beach Boys, The Mamas & The Papas, and Randy Newman were playing over the speakers. I also got a kick out of the ice cream shop being dubbed "Bur-r-r Bank Ice Cream." Of course, while this would be the most personal, it would also be only the first of several puns I would spy in the park that day.

Unfortunately, the music and puns would end up being more enjoyable for me than the park's roster of attractions. The first land we visited was Hollywood Pictures Backlot, where things started off well enough. Our first stop was the Animation Building, which, even back then, was gorgeous inside. Dozens of various sized and shaped monitors surround us as clips of some of Disney's most famous works — and *Atlantis*, for some reason — played. Sometimes these montages even included sketches or stills from the film's early production.

Following this, we visited the always enjoyable Muppet*Vision 3D. Being a huge fan of the Muppets and having not visited Disney's Hollywood Studios in some time, this was a homerun attraction for me. I remember smiling from the moment the pre-show started until I exited the main theatre. It was also pleasantly surprising to watch a 3D attraction without being whipped by rats' tails or feel bugs crawling under my rear.

Next to the Muppet's theatre was Stage 17, which was home to *Who Wants to Be a Millionaire* — Play It! Like the ABC show it was based on, the question mark was oddly absent from this incarnation as well. Anyone expecting to see Regis Philbin hosting the attraction would be sorely disappointed (although he was next door, but more on that in a minute). We took our seats in the studio and immediately investigated our answer keypads.

The show began with a "Fast Finger Round," which would be used to choose an audience member to be in the "hot seat." I don't recall what the question was, but it involved arranging four items — a, b, c, and d — in order via the keypad. When the winner of the round was announced, it turned out to be none other than my father.

Of course, this would have been more exciting if it had been the real show and not a theme park attraction considering that he would only be playing for points (which would then be traded for pins) and not actual money. Having seen the show a handful of times, my dad attempted to engage in light banter with the host instead of simply giving his answers. This included giving his rationale for each selection and using lifelines even if he didn't really need them just to keep things interesting. Admittedly, the "Phone a Complete Stranger" lifeline, which called a park guest at a nearby pay phone, was a fun twist on the real show's "Phone a Friend" bail out.

Ultimately, he went out on the question, "What network aired the XFL?" The answer (which I, of course, knew) was NBC, but he went with Fox — a somewhat reasonable guess given the networks reputation. As we exited the show, my dad rejoined us with a lanyard full of pins featuring the different point levels he had hit. At the time, I had no idea about how big pins were in the Disney world, but we were proud of him just the same.

Our Disney day took a turn as we made our way around the rest of Hollywood Pictures Backlot. Next to *Millionaire* was a large facade for a ride called Superstar Limo. The ride was deserted. So much so, that we questioned whether it was even open. However, the Cast Member at the entrance "welcomed" us in and we walked right onto our vehicle.

I'll just say it now: Superstar Limo may be the worst attraction Disney has ever built. In fact, it closed less than a year after it opened and had many of its animatronics scrapped and repurposed for Monsters Inc. Mike and Sulley to the Rescue, which opened in its place years later. The dark ride took you in a limo through the various neighborhoods of Los Angeles, meeting several celebrities along the way. Unlike Pirates of the Caribbean or even the often-criticized Ellen Degeneres audio animatronic in Ellen's

Energy Adventure, the celeb animatronics did not open their mouths or move in any lifelike manner. Instead, the "carica-tronics" (get it? Caricature animatronics) did little more than move their head and, perhaps, bounce.

Featuring Drew Carey selling star maps (what?), a trip to a tattoo parlor (huh?), and a creepy agent who kept popping up via in-vehicle TV screen (why?), the ride had more cheese than Liz Lemon's refrigerator. In fact, the only semi-clever bit in the ride was a parody of Madame Leota in the Haunted Mansion, where a head in a crystal ball said, "Agents, execs, producers beyond — Give us a sign the green light is on." It was now becoming clear that this park wasn't going to meet the high standards we had for Disney.

Granted, there were a few other attractions I enjoyed throughout the day, even if they weren't quite up to par. For example, Mulholland Madness (now Goofy's Sky School) was a fun mini-coaster that makes it feel like you are going to fly off of the switchback tracks. Having driven on Mulholland years later, I can say that this was actually themed quite well, though the ride is apparently a standard issue Wild Mouse coaster. Another enjoyable DCA 1.0 attraction that's still around is Grizzly River Rapid Run, which is perfect for a hot summer's day in Anaheim. Additionally, my family and I enjoyed the Boudin Bakery and Mission Tortilla Factory tours, and the free sourdough bread and hot tortillas that accompanied them, respectively.

And then, of course, there is Soarin' Over California. If the rest of California Adventure showed as much promise as this attraction, the park would have been a hit from the beginning. Not knowing what to expect, we took our seats only to find ourselves up against a giant IMAX-style screen moments later as it projected gorgeous scenes shot throughout the Golden State. It's no wonder that this ride still commands long lines in DCA as well as Epcot.

That day, I also took a chance and rode what was arguably the parks largest E-Ticket: California Screamin'. The grown-up coaster's track seemingly occupied the entire Paradise Pier area and featured a loop that was part of a Mickey icon at its center. This was the first (and still only) looping coaster in the Disneyland Resort and, thus, it was also the first looping coaster I had ever been on. While the shoot-off launch and loop went fine for me, the rest of the over two-and-a-half minute ride was less enjoyable.

After being nauseated by Screamin', we retreated to the nice, air-conditioned attraction Golden Dreams featuring Whoopi Goldberg. The film was great for what it was and reminded me of something you'd see in Epcot, considering it's level of "edu-tainment," Also, the replication of the Palace of Fine Arts (which remains as the entry to The Little Mermaid ~ Ariel's Undersea Adventure) was one of the parks most beautiful structures.

We skipped most of the other Paradise Pier attractions, including the Orange Stinger (a swing attraction inside of a giant, gaudy orange — rebuilt as Silly Symphony Swings), the Maliboomer (essentially Tower of Terror without any of the theming — currently replaced with a smoking area and Toy Story meet and greet), and the Golden Zephyr (which still operates... as long as there's not so much as a gentle breeze). In fact, the only other attraction we experienced that day was the Disney's Eureka! A California Parade. While I enjoyed the parade, it was definitely one of the strangest things in the park... excluding Superstar Limo.

The precession celebrated many historical events, sights, and cultures in California. Some of these things worked — like a section inspired by Hispanic culture and a marine themed float with brightly colored fish puppets. Other ideas didn't work quite as well — such as a walking Golden Gate Bridge or a guy with the Hollywood Bowl on his head.

At a certain point, we essentially shrugged our shoulders and concluded that our day had come to an end. However, I still felt unfulfilled. While I had varying levels of fun throughout the day (and more than I would have at most other places), I didn't feel like I had a Disney-level experience. For someone who looked forward to visiting Disneyland once every couple of years or so, I felt that I was cheated out of that this time.

A few days later, as we drove down the 5 (that's California speak for "Interstate 5 Freeway"), I asked my dad if we could possibly go back to "real Disneyland." To my surprise, he agreed and we went the next day. It was then that I realized what was missing from California Adventure: the story.

The reason so many kids and adults connect with Disneyland is because they're familiar with the company's films and characters. Even attractions that aren't based on films they know (Splash Mountain) or aren't based on films at all (Big Thunder Mountain Railroad) still have a clear story that adds to the overall experience. This is what elevates these rides above typical amusement park fare and into a league that few others outside of Disney could match.

As much as I love puns (and I do), a pun is not a story. Calling an attraction The Orange Stinger, housing it in an orange and shaping the seats to bee butts not only makes next to no sense but also isn't telling a story. In fact, the entire premise of the park is flawed considering that there is no explanation as to why we're in a mini-California inside of the real California.

In 2012, Disney completed their redo of Disney California Adventure and gave the park a premise with the introduction of Buena Vista Street. You would now enter to find Los Angeles as it was when Walt Disney arrived in the 1920s. The rest of the park's areas would be changed to incorporate various Disney characters and stories that were absent in the original DCA.

While it's not perfect, the California Adventure of today is a vast improvement over the one I visited in 2001 and is now a park I'm proud to have in my home resort. Disney's efforts have been rewarded by continually increasing attendance as well as great reviews from guests and media. With the mistakes of Disney's California Adventure, guests were reminded by comparison just how special Disneyland and the other Disney parks were. However, with Disney California Adventure, Disney seemingly reminded themselves that they still had that magic touch and couldn't wait to show it off to their guests once again.

17
club 33³

Like young children hearing the legend of Santa Clause, any new Disney fan comes to hear the tale of Club 33. At first it sounds like urban legend — a private club sitting over New Orleans Square, accessible only through a single door? Next comes the line, "And you can go there if you have thousands of dollars and 15 years to wait." As with many urban legends, the truth had been stretched over the years and there were many misconceptions about Club 33. The largest, in my opinion, was that you had to be a member to be able to go.

My first flirtation with Club 33 was while on the Walk in Walt's Footsteps tour that Disneyland offers. As part of the tour, you get to step past that illusive green door and into the lobby of the club. Here, you'll get to see the artwork, elevator, and stairs that the members get to see. Getting up those stairs, however, admittedly takes a bit more work.

The first time I actually got to dine at Club 33 was in September 2010. A few months prior, I had joined a podcast called *The Disneyland Gazette*.

One day we received an email from a listener named Connie (who would later join our show as well) who informed us that she could and would be willing to make us a reservation. Dispelling that "members only" rumor, not only are members allowed to make reservations for others without being present but Disney also offers company memberships that allow employees of that company to make reservations as well. This loophole is how my friends and I were able to visit that day.

Earlier in the day, D23 hosted a scavenger hunt throughout the parks. The Gazette actually broke up into three teams, although none of us proceeded to place in the rankings. Still sweaty from running around trying to answer such trivial questions like how many penguins were in the Muppet*Vision orchestra, my girlfriend (at the time) and I headed back to my car to grab our dress clothes and change in the Mickey and Friends Parking Structure restrooms.

Our party (consisting of Kenny plus kin, Luke, my girlfriend, and me) assembled at 33 Royal Street and we approached the door I had stood staring at so many times before, hoping my puppy dog eyes would catch the attention of a sympathetic Cast Member who would then give me a tour. To the left of the door is a buzzer, which I can only imagine gets rung in jest dozens of times a day. We hit the bell and, a few seconds later, a knock on the other side of the door warned us that it would soon be opening.

A Cast Member popped their head out of the barely wedged door and asked for our party's name. Passing this test felt like making it past the gatekeeper and getting to see the Wizard — "Well bust my buttons! Why didn't you say that in the first place?!" The lobby elevator, while beautiful, isn't very practical, as we had to had to break into groups of three in order to travel up to the main dining room.

Once we all made it upstairs, it took everything we had not to lag behind the host showing us to the table and explore the place instead. As we took our seats, we immediately took out our phones and cameras since the plates and menus were emblazoned with that classic 33 logo. The photos didn't let up from there and I started to feel self-conscious that we were becoming like those guests who take flash photos on Pirates of the Caribbean — the worst.

We had barely put in our orders when the temptation to step out on the balcony proved too strong. Looking across to Tom Sawyer's Island and down at the traffic of New Orleans Square, I'd never felt more special or important. I imagined others looking up and wondering, "How did they get up there? I want to go up there," as I had done so many times in the past.

As we stood on the balcony, the sun began to set, making our view even more beautiful than we could have imagined. Kenny's wife stood in the corner with a glass of red wine, looking more serene than I had ever seen a person look. The only thing that brought us back into the dining room was the fear that our nearly $100 a plate meals were getting cold.

The food was delicious, but the Club 33 experience is more about the lore and history of the place than it is the dining. Because of this, we spent nearly as much time walking around after our meal as we did eating, making sure to check out the famous Trophy Room and carefully selecting our souvenirs from the case. On that first trip, they were out of the Club 33 key chains and so I opted for the 33 ear-hat that I wore proudly out of the club and around that park that evening.

My second visit to Club 33 was nearly one year to the day after the first. It happened seemingly on a whim, as my friend just asked if I was interested in going again. I might not have been, but that particular friend owed me money from selling my Vinylmations for me and so spending that balance on dinner at 33 seemed to justify itself.

The experience was quite similar, except that this time we went for lunch. Surprisingly, I found I actually preferred the lunch service. Instead of strictly ordering off of the menu as with dinner, the lunch at Club 33 includes an appetizer and dessert bar, leaving only your main course to be ordered off of the menu.

Even though I had done it all before, my second visit was not without its magical moments. Perhaps the biggest being the revelation that one of the waiters at the club happened to be from the same small town in Scotland as one of the people in our party. What are the odds? Also notable was that the club had restocked the key chains and I was finally able to add one to my already oversized collection of keys.

I had assumed that would be my last time in Club 33... though I thought that after the first time too. However, I was proven wrong yet again the next year. At the time, I was working as an extra on *Glee* and had recently struck up a friendship with one of the recurring actresses. Somehow the topic of Club 33 came up and I, for some reason, mentioned that I thought I might be able to get us a reservation there. She informed me that 33 was on her "bucket list" and would definitely be interested should I be able to make that happen.

First, if you're not familiar with the way a television show works, I'll give you this comparison: if the show is a totem pole, with the producers and actors near the top and the production assistants at the bottom, the extras would be buried in the ground. I mean, after all, we're called "extras." An extra being able to get a principal actor into such an exclusive place as Club 33 would be a huge coup.

In a similar turnabout, I looked to another fan of our podcast who, as it turned out, was a member of Club 33. I explained the situation, and she graciously agreed to make us the reservation for the following month. When I informed the actress, she was appropriately ecstatic which, in turn, served to excite me as well.

A couple of days before our reservation, I had a minor panic attack as I realized I hadn't gotten any confirmation from the club or from the actress that we were still good to go. Of course, all this worry this was in vain and both contacted me soon after to say that everything was in place. Relieved, I took to choosing my outfit that balanced looking sharp with my desire not to melt in the Southern California sun the next day.

When we entered, I was pleased to see that everyone was as anxious to take photos and videos as I had been on my first visit. At one point, the actress even left to go the restroom, only to return seconds later saying, "Nevermind, Mickey and Pluto are heading over here and I don't want to miss them." — adorable. Additionally, when she saw a light up Tinker Bell clip on a child's drink, she requested one for herself and attached it to her complimentary glass of champagne.

Of course, doing as I normally do and overthinking everything, I started to worry about the jokes I was making about her past work. It occurred to me that I might have been coming off as some sort of stalkerish fanboy. Still, stalker or not, I got her into Club freaking 33!

Graciously, the actress picked up the check for all of six of us — a pretty penny, indeed — and, after buying more souvenirs, we met up with some of her friends in order to tour the parks together. As we made our way around, I would curiously look at other guests to see if they were looking at us and recognizing who was at the center of our entourage. We were stopped only a couple of times for people wanting photos with her, but that was really about it.

Places like Club 33 are all about status. The great irony of the club is that several of the people who get to attend don't care so much about the Disney history built into the location but are more concerned about what their membership says about their place in life. In a way, it's Disneyland's own mini-version of Los Angeles as a whole.

I've never felt comfortable with the LA scene nor was I ever 100% comfortable being in 33. Some part of me is always going to feel like a fraud that will surely be found out at any moment and escorted back out to where I belong. Although the time I spent in Club 33 was certainly exciting, I just wish I felt a little more comfortable and a lot less self-conscious so that I could enjoy those meals a bit more.

Because of the element of envy, there's really no good way to write this chapter without making people hate me. Not only did I get to go to Club 33, but I also got to go two additional times all within three years and got to take a beautiful actress one of those occasions to boot. Before that newfound hatred takes over, let me assure you that this is not meant to be braggadocios or even a "humblebrag" as the late Harris Wittels would say. This is also why I don't frequently advertise that I've been to the club (this chapter being an obvious exception). However, the reactions I get from those just learning this info are quite interesting. When people ask me about my experiences at 33, I find that the more I try to shy away from the details, the more they want to know. While they may be jealous, they also can't help but want to know all about the place they thought was mythical for so long.

In 2014, Club 33 underwent a huge remodel that not only expanded the backstage kitchen area but also re-themed areas of the club and, most notably, moved the entrance away from the famed green door on Royal Street. Call it sour grapes, but it seems to me that the new may have ruined a part of what made the club so special. To be fair, I haven't visited the new 33 for myself and, honestly, I'm not sure I'll ever have the chance to… though I have been wrong before.

I think my three times visiting Club 33 have been enough. Three visits is still three more than several fans will ever have. For all those years, I had wanted to visit for the lure and exclusivity. However, with each of those wonderful trips, I was also gifted with new friends as well as a unique experience I got to share with some my established ones. At the end of the day, those memories and friendships will last longer than any one meal at Club 33 ever could.

18
Now Exiting Fantasyland

Everyone has had a high school crush. Maybe it lasted a week, a year, or all four years of high school. Maybe it went on a little too long. Maybe it even followed you into your adult life. That's what happened to me with Ashley.

I met Ashley when I was a junior in high school and she was a freshman. We went to different schools but knew each other from our church's youth band where I played guitar and she sang. For my first attempt to hang out with her, I told her she should come see *The Lizzie McGuire Movie* with me, as it was opening that Friday. Well, I didn't actually *ask* her to go, I just mentioned it about 50 times in conversation that I was going. Understandably, she didn't come.

I've never mastered the art of discretion when it comes to my feelings and, thus, the people she dated were always wary of our friendship. The first instance was when she was dating another guy from our church named Justin. As Ashley and I got closer, Justin asked a mutual friend of ours,

Mark, to keep an eye on me and "protect" Ashley, as it were. Unfortunately for Justin (and me, I guess), when he and Ashley broke up, it was Mark whom she dated instead. During that time, there were also accusations of attempted sweetheart stealing, but I declared my innocence time and time again.

At some point, Mark and Ashley broke up as well. This conveniently left her free to go to my senior prom with me. Still, we went as friends, merely holding hands at most.

After graduating, I spent a year living about a two-hour drive away from the majority of my friends while I attended Northern Arizona University in Flagstaff, Arizona. During that time, Ashley and a couple of her friends visited once, with the three of them sleeping on the floor of my already cramped dorm room that I shared with my assigned roommate. When I returned to Phoenix at the end of the year, I accompanied one of those friends to her prom while Ashley attended with Justin, whom she had gotten back together with.

As the years went on, our friendship would go through several different levels, phases, and stages. There were times I couldn't get a hold of the girl to save my life and times when we'd pretend to be lovers for a day, making out before parting company. The times where she'd seemingly disappear from me grew longer and longer, to the point where I would write her off during each episode. Then, out of nowhere, she'd text/call me or show up at my house and reel me back in. Even a four-year absence from my life proved not long enough to truly shake her.

A year after I moved to California, Ashley got pregnant and then — as pregnant people tend to do — gave birth. A time later, I'd drive back to Arizona to visit, spending a couple of days with her and her son. During these times, I'd try to convince myself that I could help her take care of her son and the two of us could live together in Los Angeles. I was in so deep that I even wrote, directed, and cast myself in a short film that I shot the following year all about our situation and my attempts to import her to California.

In 2012, I finally got my wish. Ashley formed a plan to move to California by coming out to stay with my friend, Stephanie, for a while so she could get a job, save up some money, and find a place to live with me. Before she came, she had already lined up a handful of interviews and it seemed like things would work out well. However, despite job offers, Ashley's attitude towards the whole plan changed over the course of a week and it suddenly appeared as though she was getting ready to just head home.

On the day of my second visit to Club 33, I offered Ashley and Stephanie the free passes that were afforded to me with my club reservation. After dining, I met up with them to enjoy the parks that neither of them got to visit nearly often enough. As we walked around riding the rides and seeing the sights, I knew in the back of my mind that this would be the last time I saw Ashley for the foreseeable future. Ultimately, there was nothing California could offer her to make her stay. Not me. Not the ocean. Not even a magic kingdom.

Stephanie, who was well aware of my feelings for Ashley (having served as the hair and makeup department for the slightly fictionalized version of our story), snapped candids of us throughout the park. For the last one she took, she followed a few feet behind as Ashley and I approached the tunnels that run under the Disneyland Railroad. In the photo, Ashley (dressed in capris and a striped blouse) and I (in slacks, a pressed shirt and loosened tie) are strolling down Main Street with our arms around each other.

At the time, she may have assumed she was capturing the culmination of a long-time dream, but she had done the opposite. The photo had documented the end of the fairytale I lived in where Ashley and I somehow ended up together. Instead, she had immortalized nearly the exact moment I realized that, once past those turnstiles, this part of my life would be over.

The next morning, Ashley packed up her things and headed back to Phoenix. As Stephanie awoke to realize her absence, she called to see how I was doing, but I had already made my peace with it. To this day, I haven't seen Ashley again, though we talk from time to time and there's no ill will or bad blood between us.

I guess I had always assumed that my fairytale would come while I was in Disneyland. Instead, it arrived two years later and on the opposite coast — Walt Disney World. The first time Stephanie met my wife was when we went to Disney together. She, again, kept a few steps behind, taking photos of us holding hands throughout the park. This time, she had truly captured what she had set out to all those months before: the magic of a happily ever after.

19
Legoland

There are three times in my life that I've been so disappointed that it hurt. The first is when I saw *Ocean's Twelve* and the other two are the times I went to Legoland California. This happened twice because I thought, perhaps, changes and improvements could be made to the park since my last experience (unlike *Ocean Twelve* which, unless Steven Soderbergh releases a version with 100% more Topher Grace and 100% less Julia Roberts playing someone pretending to be Julia Roberts, will always be just as bad as I remember).

First of all, I'm a huge fan of Lego. In fact, instead of buying each other gifts for Christmas, my wife and I buy an expensive Lego set and proceeded to build the whole thing on Christmas Eve. So, naturally, the idea of a whole land of Legos was a very compelling premise to me.

Unfortunately, the major flaw of Legoland is that, unlike Disney, the attractions cater almost exclusively to children with single-digit ages. In fact, the ride that is arguably the park's largest is merely a few scenes of dark ride followed by a coaster tamer than The Barnstormer in Magic Kingdom or Gadget's Go Coaster in Disneyland. I *wish* I were exaggerating.

Interestingly, the most common phrase you hear while walking around Legoland isn't, "Gee, this is lame" or "That's it?" Instead, expect "Ohhh look, it's made out of Legos!" uttered no less than three dozen times over an eight-hour period. Somehow, the full-grown adults that make the trek down to Carlsbad, California to visit Legoland need a few good hours to truly understand the theme of the resort.

My first visit to Legoland was with my father and brother on one of our multiday California vacations. This particular trip managed to cover Disneyland, SeaWorld, the San Diego Zoo, and, due to my insistence, Legoland. At the time I remember pretending to be enjoying the experience more than I actually was so as not to seem ungrateful to my dad, who had purchased the tickets. Instead of admitting defeat, we kept trying to find the attraction that was going to win us over.

We never found it. Normally at Disney, we avoid the attraction the crowds are flocking to. However, on this day we went like lemmings into shows that would surely have to be good to draw so many people in. Unfortunately, much like real lemmings, our attempts were only met with disaster.

Years later when I moved to California, I made plans to visit a friend who had moved to San Diego just a few months before I moved to the Inland Empire. After seeing ads for some new additions to Legoland, I suggested that maybe we give the park a shot. We agreed to go mainly because she had never been and I was apparently still in denial that it could have been as bad as I recalled.

Neither of us had much money at the time, but, interestingly, this was actually a selling point for the park. Instead of the Disneyland monthly payment model that requires guests to pony up the price of a one-day admission as a down payment before breaking the rest of the cost down, Legoland divided their much-cheaper passes into even payments. This meant that I could get a year of Legoland for $11 down and $11 a month.

On top of that, the annual pass came with one free guest admission. So, to recap, instead of paying $70 each to get in, I plunked down a ten and a one so that both of us could "enjoy" a day at Legoland. Of course, those subsequent $11 monthly payments would only serve to remind me of my mistake for the rest of the year.

In the ads I saw, Legoland's latest attraction looked like Indiana Jones Adventure meets Buzz Lightyear's Astro Blasters. Had that been true, I defy anyone of you to deny the awesomeness of that ride. Alas, it turned out to be little more than their usual fare, despite the 40-minute wait we endured to experience it.

Also new since my first visit was a pirate area that had to be cool, right? *Right*?! Well, I guess if you were eight and brought a swimming suit, then yes… otherwise, not so much. And so we were still 0 for 2.

Part of me really thought I would find a whole new appreciation for the park on that visit. Instead, the only thing I found entertaining was that the arcade was named The Adventure's Club — the same as the beloved but now defunct Walt Disney World bar. Aside from that and counting the "It's made out of Legos!" people, the day was a bust. I don't remember how long we stayed, but I feel like we spent more time at the Taco Bell we went to for food after than we did in the theme park.

There's an old saying, famously butchered by President George W. Bush, that I feel really applies to this tale: Fool me once, shame on you. Fool me twice, shame on me. To this day, I still get e-mail offers from Legoland since I was once an annual passholder. I quickly delete these messages lest I fall for a trifecta of trickery. Despite my success on this front so far, there is the very real possibility that my curiosity will one day get the best of me and I'll visit the relatively new Legoland Orlando in the future.

If anything ever does get me to a return to Legoland, it will almost un-doubtedly be related to *The Lego Movie*, which was practically perfect in every way. That film's theme, "Everything is Awesome," certainly wouldn't apply to Legoland in my opinion, but it's also clear the park wasn't built for me. Instead, perhaps the lyrics should go, "Everything is awesome/Everything is cool when you're under age three." But, if *The Lego Movie* taught us anything, it's that kids and adults should be able to have fun and play together… where have I heard that idea before?

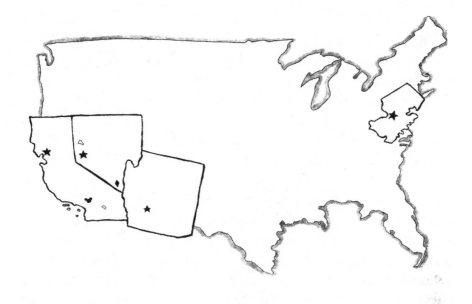

20
Suburban Legends
and the Christmas World Tour

Admittedly, I wish I could take credit for such a clever title as "Suburban Legends," but it belongs to the band this story is about. I have seen Suburban Legends perform more times than any other band, outside of church. The funny thing is that no matter how many times I see them or listen to their songs, I never get tired of them.

The first time I saw Suburban Legends was on July 17th (Disneyland's birthday) in 2004, just after I had graduated high school. Reel Big Fish and Rx Bandits were performing at the House of Blues Anaheim in Downtown Disney and I just happened to be in town for my family's annual So Cal trip. This may come as a surprise to you, but my father and I share similar taste in music. As a result, he has accompanied me to many Warped Tours, concerts, and punk rock shows over the years. While he wasn't too familiar with Reel Big Fish outside of their radio singles, my interest was enough to pique his.

If you've never been, the House of Blues is an intimate-to-midsized venue with two levels. The floor usually gets crowded and cramped quickly, so my father and I instead found spots along the railing of the balcony. From there, I watched as Suburban Legends' horn section got onto each other's shoulders to engage in a mock robot fight, danced around the stage, and performed Disney covers. Needless to say, I was hooked.

It would be years before I saw them perform again. Five years later, when I moved to Rancho Cucamonga (yes, that is a real place), I planned to celebrate my relocation with a visit to Disneyland that weekend. To my surprise and delight, Suburban Legends were performing at Tomorrowland Terrace. At the time, the area was being referred to as the TLT Dance Club as part of Summer Nightastic. This essentially just meant that TV screens that would display text messages sent in by park-goers were added and that each one the band's sets were introduced by a girl dressed like she was straight of '87.

The band was every bit as great as I remembered and I soon made it a point to head to Anaheim any time they were performing. Apparently I wasn't the only one, as I recognized the same core of a dozen or so people that would be in front of the stage every time I arrived. Another time, a friend and I even took a day trip to Las Vegas to see them play at another House of Blues with Goldfinger and, once again, Reel Big Fish.

Suburban Legends became part of a lot of my holiday plans as well. Since they typically played sets at Tomorrowland Terrace on the Fourth of July and New Year's Eve, I'd often just make heading to TLT after work on those days my default itinerary. While their sets are always fun, tight, and full of energy, one of their shows remains the most memorable for me: New Year's Eve, 2010.

The August prior, I had left my full time job as movie theater manager, freeing me up to actually travel for the holidays for the first time in six years. As a result, my presence was requested in several places. Instead of spending a nice, relaxing holiday at home, it quickly became apparent that I was going to have to travel around the country.

When I was 12 years old, my parents divorced. A few years later, my mother moved to Las Vegas while my father stayed in Phoenix. In March of 2010, he remarried and so this was to be his first holiday season with his new wife and her two daughters. While my younger brother, Scott, and my stepsister, Stacie, still lived in Phoenix, my other stepsister, Wendi, lived in Michigan. Wendi had booked her trip to come home for the holidays and, when I finally announced to my family that I had left my job, it was hoped that I too would visit Arizona so we could have a good ol' fashioned family portrait done while all four kids were actually in the same place.

Meanwhile, my mother had made plans to visit her family in New Jersey. Even before I left my job, she had requested that my brother and I come along. This was especially important to her as my grandmother's Alzheimer's had progressed and the family (correctly) anticipated that this Christmas would be her last.

Not wanting to disappoint either of my parents, I devised what I called my Christmas World Tour: 2010 edition. The plan was that I would first drive from California to my mother's house in Las Vegas. From there, we would fly to New Jersey, where she would stay with my grandparents and I would stay with my cousin. Then, after flying back to Las Vegas, I would drive down to Arizona before Wendi flew home in order to get our family portrait. Finally, I planned to drive through to Anaheim from Phoenix for New Year's Eve, thus completing my tour. Four cities, one week — world tour!

Predictably, since I had made a plan, God had laughed. First, as I had feared, my grandmother had no idea who I was. It would take about 15 minutes to explain to her how we were related... and she'd forget approximately 10 minutes later. She got as far as to understand that I was Charlie's grandson and that she was Charlie's wife but couldn't grasp why that meant that she should know me.

After days of this depressing version of "Who's On First," God continued to laugh as New Jersey was hit by a blizzard. The storm effectively shut down Newark Airport, which I was supposed to fly out of two days later. Having not seen snow since I spent a year in Flagstaff, Arizona for school, it was fun to play in the powder and make snow angels... for about an hour. After that, I was ready to get the heck out.

Leaving town would, of course, prove quite difficult, seeing as Newark Liberty had been closed for a day and a half. We arrived to EWR on time for a flight that would *surely* not be leaving on time and the terminal looked like what I would imagine Disneyland would after some mysterious virus outbreak: long lines and zombies. After an hour in line just to see the counter agent to check in (the online check in was down and the "help line" for the airline would have been more helpful if they had just given me a big middle finger), I was given a boarding pass without a seat assignment.

Following another hour or so in line at security, I was safely at my gate wondering if I would even get to go on the plane. Somehow, my mother and her girlfriend both had seat assignments. I threatened that, if for some reason she got on the plane and I didn't, her current role of "mother" would have to be recast. After all, this was her brilliant idea to visit New Jersey — a state we had incidentally moved away from following a giant blizzard.

I eventually got a seat assignment and our flight departed only a few hours late. After a short nap at my mom's house, I packed up my stage gear and pointed the tour bus towards Phoenix. Seemingly out of spite, it was raining when I arrived. Aside from that, this leg of the tour was pretty easy and I was off to Anaheim for the grand finale.

Not surprisingly, Disneyland was packed for the New Year's festivities. After a few laps around the parks, I made my way to Tomorrowland Terrace, where I stayed for the rest of the evening. Suburban Legends rocked it as always, covering "Under the Sea," "I Just Can't Wait to Be King," and "DuckTales" in addition to their numerous originals.

As the countdown began, and the fireworks appeared above the Matterhorn, I thought about the week I had just endured. Sure I love my family and I was happy to see them for the holidays, but my so-called "tour" had taken its toll me. I had spent that week flying around the country trying to make everyone else happy. So now, as the New Year rang in, I resolved to take this night for myself and what I wanted to do was watch Suburban Legends play some of my favorite songs. On that night, there was nowhere else in the world I'd rather have been.

21
Super Fan, Super Fail

Once I reconnected with Suburban Legends after becoming a Disneyland local, I caught up by buying all of the albums, following them on Twitter, and, of course, going to all of their shows. As part of this process, I had also learned a decent amount about each of the band's members and the history of the group. However, one thing I certainly didn't know was that my cousin was actually friends with several of them.

My cousin, Kristin, had been planning to move back to Los Angeles from New Jersey around the same time that I moved. On one occasion, she was in town to make sure that all went smoothly. Knowing that I was always up for a trip to Disney, she asked me and another one of her friends to take her to the parks and show her around.

Since I had the Premium pass that allowed me to park for free and she was saving all her money for her move, we met up at Brea Mall so that we could carpool the rest of the way. After we all loaded into my car and we pulled out of the parking lot, I heard her friend giggle from the backseat. Looking in the rear view mirror, I saw her holding up one of my Suburban Legends CDs. Well, not just any CD — this one was a special version of their EP *Dance Like Nobody's Watching* which had been subtitled *Tokyo Nights* and was only released in Japan. I had spent a good portion of my trip to Tokyo tracking it down and it took at least a dozen record stores before I finally found it. Like I said, I'm a fan.

She got my cousin's attention and she proceeded to laugh as well. I couldn't help but wonder what inside joke I was being left out of. Her friend asked if I liked the band, to which I pointed out the *Tokyo Nights* subtitle and condescendingly filled her in on the label's significance the way a wine snob might romanticize a vintage red.

Upon finishing my rather admittedly dorky tale, she informed me that we would most likely be meeting up with Brian Klemm, the guitarist for the band, in the parks that day. Apparently the two went way back and my cousin had also become friends with him during her first stint in California. I looked down only realize that I was also wearing a Suburban Legends t-shirt.

Part of me thought that perhaps no one would notice this faux pas considering that the shirt was mostly just a blue green swirl that could almost be anything. However, when we did meet up with Brian, he immediately recognized my shirt. So much for that... My cousin made a point of throwing me under the bus further by telling him that tale of my import record. Luckily, he sounded genuinely impressed and flattered instead of, ya know… horrified and concerned.

The rest of the day, Kristin would look over to me as if she expected me to burst with fanboy excitement at any moment. I played it cool because, at this point, I had worked with my favorite actors on my favorite television shows and gotten paid for it, so I had learned not to let such things faze me. Still, I will admit that it was pretty cool to get to hang out with someone I admired so much — especially at Disneyland, of all places — even if it was somewhat embarrassing.

Since then, I've actually run into him in the parks a couple of other times… and it's never *not* been awkward. One time I ran into him while I was with my friend, Charlotte. Oddly, he just seen me a couple of nights earlier when he turned up at the bar Kristin worked at for "grilled cheese night" — the only time you'd ever be able to find me at a bar. Recognizing me from mere hours earlier, we stopped for a moment and chatted. As we were about to part, Charlotte politely said that maybe we could meet up later and suggested that I text him with our whereabouts. I then had to explain to her that we weren't *actually* friends. No, I was just a fan, and that was all right with me.

22
Top Ten

In September 2012, my good friend Chris was faced with a predicament: he was going to find himself in Tokyo for work, but would only have two days to spend at the Tokyo Disneyland Resort. Chris is the type of guy who wants to dig into each park he visits as deep as he does when he's at his home resort in Anaheim. Of course, this wouldn't be possible if he only had one day to explore each of the Tokyo parks.

The mere idea of not being able to see everything proved so stressful that he even considered not going at all. To calm him, I proposed that he had to visit the parks for the two days that he could but that this would just be a "preview visit." I assured him that he'd return to Tokyo someday in the relatively near future and could delve deeper then. Additionally, I armed him with a cheat sheet I called my "Tokyo Top Ten." This way, he would know which attractions were worth his precious Tokyo time and which were little more than domestic clones.

When I originally created this list for him, it was based on my visit in

2010. On that trip, I didn't get to see Monsters Inc. Ride and Go Seek or Aquatopia since they were under refurbishment. Additionally, Toy Story Mania, Philharmagic and Fantasmic weren't yet open. Also since his visit, the Under the Sea has undergone major changes and is no longer the show that either of us ended up seeing. Finally, Dreamlights has gone through a number of changes but remains just as awesome as ever.

Here is the list I presented to Chris to help him on his abbreviated journey:

Tokyo Top Ten

1) **Pooh's Hunny Hunt**: Trackless ride system = Wow. You get different experiences based on train position. Grab a FastPass or go there first because it's usually the park's longest line

2) **Mysterious Island/Journey to the Center of the Earth**: Try to breathe when you first enter this area — it's impossible. Great ride, but closes frequently since it's the same system as Test Track.

3) **Mermaid Lagoon/Under the Sea**: Lovely themed and gorgeous inside. There aren't any rides you'll need to do inside, but *do not* miss Under the Sea. It's an incredibly creative show I still have trouble describing to this day and, since photography is forbidden, no one will know how awesome it really is. I can't wait to discuss this with you after.

4) **Sindbad's Storybook Voyage**: You walk in expecting a three-minute dark-ride and instead are treated to a 10-minute, Pirates of the Caribbean level adventure. Not to mention, an incredible song by Alan Menken I fell in love with in spite of the fact that I couldn't understand more than four words.

5) **Tokyo Disneyland Electrical Parade - Dreamlights**: Remember World Four from Super Mario? Where everything was *huge*? That's what this parade is like compared to Main Street Electrical Parade. Great new floats and super sized versions of some classics. Only in Tokyo.

6) **Critter Country**: A single ride (Splash Mountain) resides in this town, but unlike our dead end land, Tokyo's critter country is an independent hill full of burrows and tunnels that turn guests into critters themselves.

7) **Tower of Terror**: Florida has the fifth dimension, but I vastly prefer this version's story, effects, and drop sequence. It's literally one of a kind.

8) **The Enchanted Tiki Room - Stitch Presents Aloha e Komo Mai!**: Again, it's all in Japanese, but this show is extremely enjoyable. If, God forbid, our show ever left, I declare this to be an acceptable replacement (it's no Under New Management).

9) **Indiana Jones Adventure- Temple of the Crystal Skull**: Yes, it's pretty close to ours, but don't miss your chance to see the great alternate scenes in their version. Also, thankfully, it has nothing to do with the fourth Indy film.

10) **StormRider**: A fun simulator ride. Not overly amazing, but it is a Tokyo exclusive.

Honorable Mention- Country Bear Jamboree: ...in Japanese?! Well, the songs are in mostly English, but having the narration in a different language is a fun twist on a classic.

23
Islands of Misadventure

For the past few years, it has been argued by some that Universal was surpassing Disney in quality of attractions. This, of course, came about after the opening of The Wizarding World of Harry Potter, which is based on the massively successful films, which, in turn, were based on the proportionately successful books. Whether I agreed with this notion or not, it was clear that I needed to visit for myself.

My trip to Universal almost didn't happen as I had waffled on the idea of going since I had arrived in Florida. Considering that I already had a pass for Walt Disney World, it seemed silly for me to spend more money to go to another theme park other that the one I was in town for. In fact, my friend Aaron and I didn't actually decide to go until we woke up that morning and said, "Well I suppose we should."

For all of my complaining about spending extra money, I ended up buying a park hopper — I mean a "Park-to-Park Admission ticket," mainly so that I could relive my childhood memories of E.T. Adventure. Aside from that, Universal Studios proper had little to offer me since we have versions of The Simpson's Ride and Revenge of the Mummy at Universal Studios Hollywood. And so it was time for my first adventure to the Islands.

Unlike the somewhat-similarly titled Disney California Adventure, Islands of Adventure is a theme that encompasses a lot… even if the "Islands" portion of the name remains inconsequential for the most part. From comic strips to *Jurassic Park* and Dr. Seuss to *Harry Potter*, the park admittedly holds something for everyone. Its other claim to fame is being home to several Marvel attractions that were built before Disney bought the comic giant and, thus, served to confuse the entire Orlando theme park market and the guests who visited them.

Upon entering the park, we did what I'd estimate 80% of guests visiting after 2010 have done and headed straight towards The Wizarding World of Harry Potter. By the time we got to Hogsmeade, it was clear that a ride on the land's signature attraction — Harry Potter and the Forbidden Journey — was out of the question unless we felt like investing multiple hours of time off the bat. Instead, Aaron gave me a brief tour of the town and I took the opportunity to snap photos of the insanely convincing Hogwarts Castle.

As you exit the Wizarding World, you end up on Isla Nublar — otherwise known as the home of Jurassic Park. Though Universal Studios Hollywood also has a version of what Islands of Adventure calls the Jurassic Park River Adventure, one thing Hollywood doesn't have is the Pherandon Flyers which circle high above the "island." Unfortunately, Aaron and I were not able to navigate one of these dinos as the park requires all riders to be accompanied by a child. After considering everything from kidnapping to having Aaron lawyer the ride operators on the grounds of ageism, we opted to just let it go and move on instead.

Following a full tour of IoA, we popped over to Universal Studios Hollywood for a ride on the aforementioned E.T. attraction. Incidentally, I never liked the film *E.T.* as a kid, mainly because the scene where the "loveable" alien gets drunk deeply upset me as a youngster. But anyone who loves Reese's Pieces as much as he does is a friend of mine.

Aside from the confusing pre-show that blurs the storyline of the attraction, E.T. Adventure is as close to a Disney-level attraction (pre-Potter) as I can think of. Starting with the incredible queue that truly sets the scene, the entire experience still holds up. OK, maybe E.T.'s home planet is bit cheesy and weird, but I give it a pass if for no other reason than it's preceded by one of my favorite scenes in any dark ride — the launch over the cop car and into the air.

I've often made fun of the fact that nearly every Universal attraction (at least in Hollywood) makes use of water as an effect, I learned from my venture east that the company also has a strange spinning fetish. From the moderately fun Men in Black ride in Studios to the started-off-great-but-died-fast Cat in the Hat dark ride, the motion was as unnecessary and it was nauseating. To be fair, the latter attraction has apparently removed a considerable amount of this in the years since my visit.

At some point during the day, I dragged Aaron on Dudley Do-Right's Ripsaw Falls mainly because of my infatuation with The Rocky and Bullwinkle Show. Though it held a posted wait time of 60 minutes, we were in our vehicles within 20 minutes (ah, the classic Universal over-post). While the ride was certainly enjoyable, Aaron and I couldn't believe how soaked we had gotten. Clearly they really wanted us to pay the $5 to enter the giant heaters that stood near the attraction's entrance.

With soaked jeans, we exited the attraction (which still said it was a 60 minute wait — lies) and discussed what was next for us. We bypassed those tempting dyers and instead made our way to the nearby Popeye and Bluto's Bilge-Rat Barges figuring that we couldn't possibly be any damper than we already were. If you're already laughing, I've either properly foreshadowed the stupidity of that notion or you've been there.

You know how on Grizzly River Rapid Run or Kali River Rapids the streams of water that hit you are light and playfully pleasant? Not so on Popeye's ride. Aside from the frequent buckets of water our boat would take on, the water that was shot at us both from the attraction as well as sadists off its shore felt like a kid had spent half a day pumping their top of the line Super Soaker before blasting you with it at point blank range. Believe me when I tell you it was actually painful.

I came off of the ride conservatively weighing five pounds more than I did when I foolishly volunteered myself to the attraction. Leaving a trail of water behind us, we chased what little sun there was left before it set for the evening leave us high and… well, not dry. Universal *still* did not get my $5, but it was a darn good try.

We were still soaked by the time our table at Mythos was ready. I had heard a lot about the restaurant over the years, mostly because — as they proudly display on a banner out front — it was voted Best Theme Park Restaurant six years in a row by Theme Park Insider. That's why Aaron and I were so surprised to see that the entrées were all reasonably priced considering that "Best Theme Park Restaurant" would place it above all of the amazing Epcot eateries, which surely cost more than this.

So is Mythos really that good? Well, it's not bad... but "best" is a bit strong. Aaron and I concluded that such a statement would have to be based on a rubric as opposed to just straight-up quality. I guess if you were weighing theme, value, and service then Mythos would score pretty well. Still, I have to believe that the "best" theme park restaurant would be able to remove ingredients from my dish by request, which Mythos was not. Despite that, my panini was still delicious (even with the peppers and onions I'm usually opposed to), our waitress was incredibly friendly, and no one judged me for leaving a puddle on my chair — yup, I was still dripping wet. That Popeye... Why I oughta...

Our final stop of the night was back in the Wizarding World for my first ride on Forbidden Journey and some Butterbeer for dessert. I can't think of many attractions where the queue is more impressive than the ride itself, but Harry Potter and Forbidden Journey qualifies for me. This isn't to say the ride is weak by any means, but getting to explore Hogwarts could easily be an attraction in itself (and apparently is in Universal Studios Japan).

As for the actual ride, it's hard to properly review an attraction when my eyes were closed for a good portion of it. It started off well enough, but the womping willows and Dementors startled me so badly I thought I might wet myself... not that anyone would have been able to tell the difference given the state of my pants at that point. By the time my Kooka arm placed me back down, I was glad I had experienced the attraction but had no desire to do so again. Unfortunately, the ride also left me with a nice headache to take home.

Luckily, I was still feeling well enough for Butterbeer — a drink I was beginning to think people enjoyed more than the actual land. I'm not normally a fan of butterscotch, but I enjoyed the beverage regardless. In fact, my only regret is that they were not serving it warm like they have been with the introduction of Diagon Alley.

The one positive thing about Universal's early closing hour of 9 P.M. is that Aaron and I were able to quickly change our clothes at his apartment and head over to the Magic Kingdom before it closed at 1 A.M. While there, we discussed the pros and cons of Universal. Our biggest pro was that the resort as a whole is a fun place to hang out and does have a number of great attractions. However, our main problem with Universal is the nickel and diming that occurs throughout the day. Good luck purchasing a one-day, one-park ticket; you'll sit through a 10 minute spiel about adding days, adding dining, or upgrading to an Express pass that allows you to cut the lines (the sale of which I presume is partially spurred by the frequent over posting of wait times).

Die-hard Universal fans routinely mock "pixie-dusters" for their un-wavering allegiance to the Mouse and many Disney loyalists are quick to make Universal a punch line when speaking of Disney's strengths and weaknesses. Though the two resorts are competitors, the market is plenty big enough for the both of them. Theme park fans would be completely remiss to skip Universal during their trips to Central Florida, especially following the Diagon Alley expansion of The Wizarding World of Harry Potter, which I have seen and is amazing. While I may have been hard on Universal in this story for comical effect, the truth is that I do enjoy their parks.

So is Universal surpassing Disney? I'd have to give a resounding "no" to that question. I don't think any theme park will ever overtake the masters. Not only does Disney win in terms of theme and experience but also in guest service and quality. However, I'd be more than happy to watch Universal try to beat them at their own. After all, a rising tide lifts all boats… just make sure Popeye isn't aboard any of those vessels.

24
Duffy

A couple of years before Disney's nautical-adventuring bear made his way to the states, Duffy was — like so many American one-hit-wonders — huge in Japan. This is a fact I was unaware of upon arriving at Tokyo DisneySea. I suppose I had seen girls in Tokyo Disneyland the day before carrying teddy bears dressed in various clothes, but this didn't really catch me as odd.

Cut to me entering American Waterfront for the first time and spying a store named McDuck's. Being a hopeless 90's kid, I dreamt that inside would be a trove of Disney Afternoon collectibles and t-shirts. I even imagined the possibility of there being a faithful recreation of the character's gold coin swimming pool, as featured in the opening titles. This may seem quite far-fetched, but if anyone could pull off such a thing it would be the Japanese.

Unfortunately for Huey, Dewey, Louie, and me, the store featured none of these things. Instead, I was surrounded by nothing but seemingly generic stuffed bears. At first I figured this had to be some mistake, as the place was so jammed that it was almost hard to navigate. I thought the gold coin pool must be towards the back and that's why everyone was over there. But, alas, nothing but stuffed animals and ridiculous outfits lined the shelves. Despite the absence of lions or tigers, I still let out an, "Oh my," at the sight of all these bears, though in a far more disgusted tone than that of Dorothy and her friends.

With hopes dashed, I exited the store and made my way down the rest of the 1920s New York-themed street when something at the end of block caught my eye: a full-sized version of the very bear that occupied my would-be DuckTales-themed boutique! The line to meet him was of a length usually reserved for a new princess and each girl in line proudly held miniature versions of him. While the shop offered dozens if not hundreds of wardrobe options, this full-sized version sported a sailor's hat, shirt, and tie. I briefly considered waiting in line just to ask him where Bear Tennille was, but I assumed the joke wouldn't land since it's 40 years too late and not very funny.

Around the corner, the New York theme ended and a Cape Cod area emerged. This change in scenery did not mean the end of our new bear friend, however, as he had his own popcorn stand flavor (milk tea), souvenir bucket, and even restaurant. At this point I wondered if anyone from the Oriental Land Company had ever even been to Massachusetts.

Thankfully, the rest of the park was more or less bear free. I learned later in the day (probably on my second or third stroll around the park to get a sense of the place) that the bear's name was Duffy. It took another whole day to realize that the lighter portion of his face made a Mickey icon. Even though I could tell that this Duffy fellow was pretty popular, it never once crossed my mind that he was some sort of phenomenon that I should bring home in order to expose his wonder to all my friends.

Alas, I missed my chance to be a Duffy hipster as, a couple years later, it was announced that Duffy would be making his way over to Disney California Adventure and Epcot. Immediately, I went to all the people I had discussed my Tokyo trip with and retroactively informed them what a big deal he was over there and that I can't believe I had forgotten to mention him. You'll recall that I never did go wait in line to meet Duffy that day in the American Waterfront, but that didn't stop me from lying to the poor bear's face when I met him in California Adventure a few months after his arrival.

"I met you in Tokyo! I'm so glad you're here now!"

25
Peter Pan's Flight

Perhaps the question most frequently asked of Disney fans is, "What is your favorite attraction?" I've found that speaking on the pros and cons of two or three attractions (not to mention clarifying whether they meant a ride or a show) usually leads to the follow up, "Yeah, but what is your *favorite*?" Because of this, I have honed my definitive answer: Peter Pan's Flight.

More specifically, I'm partial to the Disneyland version of the attraction not because it resides in my home resort but because of the lovely flight over Neverland complete with fiber optic stars that's lacking in other incarnations of the ride. Admittedly, in a perfect world, a longer version of the flight would be created that gives us the great aerial view of the island as seen in the original before sailing in for the up-close tour found in the Magic Kingdom version. Still, given the choice between the two, I have to say that the simple yet spectacular sight found in Anaheim makes the ride for me.

I suspect that many Disney fans find themselves relating to the story of *Peter Pan*. Given that the park experience is intended to instill the feeling of being a kid in those of an older age, it makes sense that a tale with a protagonist who doesn't wish to ever grow up would be appealing. Whether subconsciously or not, perhaps that's what originally attracted me to this ride.

Within today's society, the Peter Pan comparison for the young at heart has been somewhat sullied. Not only does the term "Neverland" now call to mind the late Michael Jackson and the various scandals surrounding the pop singer but the idea of Pan is also frequently lobbed as a criticism of the Millennial generation that I am begrudgingly a member of. In fact, of all the names for this sect of the population (commonly referred to as "Generation Y" before the Millennial tag caught on) "The Peter Pan Generation" is actually a widely used one. While part of me is flattered that there's a Disney allusion contained in my generation's nickname, the truth is that this is not intended as a compliment.

The knock on The Peter Pan Generation is that we tend to put off many of life's milestones that our parents achieved at much younger ages like getting married and having kids. Ironically, since I was about 21 or so, my plan was to propose to whomever I would marry while flying over the aforementioned Neverland scene I loved so much. Even more ironically, I read years later that someone else had done just that. Great minds...

I guess Peter Pan is really more of a divisive character than many of us realize. In a way, I feel as though Peter shares some qualities with television's Archie Bunker. On *All in the Family*, Archie's beliefs and rants are often misguided. However, the intention is not for the audience to take Bunker's lessons at face value, but instead to inform us that we should strive to do the opposite of the character.

Similarly, we learn from Pan that, as much as we sometimes resist growing up, it's not only inevitable but also 100% necessary. It's also worth noting that, upon re-watching the Disney film, you may find Peter severely less likable than you recall him being when you were kid. Though his antics may have been entertaining to our youthful sensibilities, as adults we are able to see the flaws in his petulance and even take issue with his behavior.

Despite all this, Peter Pan's Flight remains a gorgeous and impressive attraction (even if it is only two minutes long). I'd argue that the true reason for the constant lines the ride attracts on both coasts is because of these qualities. To be sure, the 20:1 wait to ride time ratio is a bit steep, but I've never once regretted my decision to embark on my Neverland-bound sailing ship.

As I'm writing this, Peter Pan's Flight in Disneyland is undergoing a refurbishment. Rumors are that this redo will add many of the impressive effects that were brought to Alice in Wonderland only a few months prior. While the additions to Alice bring a whole new level to the ride, I do fear that my favorite part of Pan's attraction will be lost to the modern make-over. Although I still have faith and trust (you'll have to look elsewhere for pixie dust) that the Imagineers will see things my way, the truth is that they may not. Should that be the case, I'll just have to remember what Peter — perhaps inadvertently — taught me: change may be difficult, but it's needed.

26
CM

In my explorations to find a career that truly made me happy, several friends would ask why I didn't apply to work at Disneyland. They said this as though the possibility had never occurred to me. To them, it made perfect sense: I love Disneyland, so why wouldn't I want to work there? My answer has always been the same: I wouldn't want to ruin the magic.

When I was a child, I used to think that movie theaters were magical. The neon lights, the big auditoriums, the sound of the projector you could hear from the back row. But then when I turned 16, I got hired at a nearby theatre. I soon learned that once you step onto the other side of that concession stand, clean up after a sold out show, or get eviscerated by a guest for something that is not your fault, the magic is effectively gone.

I have several friends who are Cast Members and each of them love it. To them, the magic they may lose from seeing the other side of the parks is easily replenished by the magic they create for others on a daily basis.

Not to mention, being a Cast Member makes a Disney obsession far more affordable.

Part of me likes to think that I too could be like them, but I really don't think I could. Perhaps I could see myself as a tour guide or maybe even Jungle Cruise Skipper, but that's about it. This isn't to say I look down on Cast Members. On the contrary, I find their job to be extremely difficult and commend them for doing it so well.

Cast Members are called as such because they are part of a show and are acting while on stage. Guest Service Cast Members smile when they really want to punch you, attractions Cast Members deliver their, "Unfortunately, the Yeti is sleeping" line with the same level of empathy to every child who asks why the Matterhorn is closed, and every outdoor cart vendor dances along to song as the parade rolls by them as if it really were the best part of their day. Like method actors, the best Cast Members become their roles and grow to love what they do. Together, the Cast Members of the Disney parks put on the greatest show on earth every single day — despite what the circus may claim.

When I still lived in Arizona and worked at the movie theatre, my district manager asked me to do a report on Disney's guest service. Naturally, I saw the project as an excuse to skip town and head to Disneyland. As I stood admiring the sight of the bay near what was then The Sun Wheel, an off-duty Cast Member joined me and we started to chat.

As our conversation progressed, I got up the nerve to tell him about my assignment and ask him what he could tell me about their guest service training. Immediately, he took out a small card that had The Four Keys written on them: safety, courtesy, show, and efficiency. He explained them all to me and how the order was specific to the importance of each. Afterwards, he even let me keep the card and I thanked him for his help.

During our conversion, I told him that I was thinking of moving to California (which he endorsed) I learned that he had worked at Disneyland before coming across the esplanade to open Disney's California Adventure. This means that he had spent over a decade with the company at that point. Since he seemed genuinely happy with what he did in life, I sheepishly inquired if his job ever ruined the magic for him. His response was simple, "Not if you don't let it."

That phrase has really stuck with me over the years. So much so, that

I've even reconsidered my position on the whole matter. Still, I don't quite think I could bring myself to ever become a Disney Cast Member, but I'll forever be thankful to those who do.

27
Swishes

In March of 2012, my Disneyland Premium Passport was set to expire. As I had for the past five years, I spent a good amount of time contemplating all of my pass renewal options before, inevitably, deciding just to keep my no-block out, free parking, 20% discount, Premium. However, this was the year right after my friend, Aaron, had relocated to Orlando, leading me to believe that some cheap Walt Disney World trips were in my near-future.

With this in mind, I began looking into the Premier Passport, which Disney had launched just one-year prior. The new pass acted as a Premium Passport at both the Disneyland Resort as well as the Walt Disney World Resort. While the pass definitely existed, information on it seemed to hide in the deep web of Disney websites and wasn't even advertised on property. After working my way through pages and pages of message board threads, I learned that I could essentially add four extra parks — not to mention two water parks and DisneyQuest — to my measly two-park pass for a scant $250.

Once this was a done deal, I immediately informed Aaron that he was going to have company. Wasting no time, I planned my visit for only a couple of weeks later. This, of course, fell right into the heart of Spring Break season, meaning that I would have to endure large crowds in the parks. However, I learned that there was at least one plus to this attendance spike: long operating hours.

Because of these crowds, we would, as a rule, avoid Magic Kingdom during the day. Instead, we would arrive around 9 A.M. at the earliest and stay until the parks 1 A.M. close. Though the park would eventually empty out around 11, our nearly perfect plan was often foiled by Magic Kingdom's back to back to back entertainment block that tended to kick off just as we would enter.

Fighting our way up Main Street, we bailed left, entering Adventureland. Unlike Disneyland's Adventureland, Magic Kingdom's is a wide open oasis that stood in sharp contrast to the packed Main Street we had just come from and provided us with ample room for such tasks as walking or breathing. As we continued on our short stroll — enjoying the ability to take five paces forward without having our heels clipped by a stroller — we passed the Swiss Family Robinson Treehouse. I stopped and stared for a moment for two reasons: 1) Disneyland's Treehouse had been taken over by Tarzan years before, so I'm always up for reliving the original 2) The fireworks were about to begin and I had an idea. Turning to Aaron, I asked if the attraction remained open during the fireworks. To my surprise, he didn't know, but we resolved to find out.

To paraphrase Dr. Ian Malcolm, we were so preoccupied with, "*Could we do this?*" that we never stopped to think, "*Should we do this?*" We soon discovered you could, indeed, watch Wishes from the Swiss Family Robinson Treehouse. As you climb up, there is only one spot near the paramount of the steps that allows the height and angle necessary to see Cinderella Castle and the fireworks.

We weren't the only ones who had this supposedly brilliant idea, as another family had already found this landing and occupied it. As a result, we chose to stand on a set of stairs just up where they were standing. Our timing was near perfect. Just as we got settled, the lights went out and the music began: "Wishes!/ Dream a dream/ Wishes!" While this wasn't the best angle, the fireworks were in clear view and the quarters were not as cramped as those in the hub where all the normal people were enjoying the show.

As the Jiminy Cricket narration kicked in, we noticed something odd: the Swisskapolka, which emanated from a turntable only a few steps down from our prime spot, was still playing. A few moments later, the sound stopped and we breathed a sigh of relief. However, less than a minute later, the music started it's loop once more. At this point, the family near us threw in the towel and continued their adventure through the Treehouse.

We remained through the rest of the show, viewing a special remix of Wishes we so cleverly dubbed "Swishes." "Swishes!/ Dream a dream/ Swishes!" This led to the idea of adding "Swisskapolka" to other Disney shows and attractions. Imagine the "Swisskaroque Hoedown" (or "Barolka Hoedown") in Disney's Electrical Parade, Swiss's Great Escape in Tomorrowland (honestly, an improvement), or even Swiss Mountain (either Splash or Space, and, incidentally, not the Matterhorn).

Unfortunately, we never did get around to attempting those other remixes. We did, however, invite our friends to their own private viewing of Swishes the next evening. To celebrate the occasion, we began replacing every "wish" with "swish" during the program: "We'll make a swish and do as dreamers do/ And all our swishes will come true."

28
NYEpcot

For New Year's Eve 2012, I varied my tradition of celebrating in Disneyland slightly by, instead, spending the holiday in Walt Disney World. Wanting to help justify my expensive Premier Passport purchase, I asked — nay — told Aaron that I was going to work in a second trip before the year's end. After agreeing to my demand (as if he had a choice), he suggested I try December because his favorite artist, Amy Grant, was going to be hosting Candlelight Processional towards the end of the month. Additionally, he and some friends had already made reservations at Garden Grill as part of a package that would grant them priority seating to Candlelight and happened to have one extra spot available. That was reason enough for me and so it was then settled that I would visit just after Christmas and stay until the beginning of the new year.

The night of our reservation, we waited at the Land Pavilion to meet up with Aaron's friends, Reuben and Rebekah, both of whom I had met briefly during my visit earlier in the year. Reuben was the first to greet us and Rebekah (running late, per her reputation) arrived a bit after. After apologizing away her tardiness, Rebekah turned to me and said, "I thought you killed yourself." As she added the next line, "That wasn't you?" Aaron and Reuben looked on horrified, apparently missing the reference to *Garden State* — one of my favorite films that I actually have a tattoo of on my arm. Once the air was cleared, we headed on into the rotating restaurant and took our seats.

Dinner was more enjoyable than expected given my affliction to vegetables and the restaurant being called "Garden Grill" — "Some more of the steak and mashed potatoes, please" was a frequently used phrase at our table. Time flew by during dinner and, when we looked at our watches (who are kidding? They were cell phones), soon realized it was nearly showtime. After paying our bill, we rushed over to America Gardens only to find ourselves caught in pouring rain.

Perhaps ordering that last round of steak and potatoes or embarking on the hidden Mickey scavenger hunt our waiter roped us into were mistakes, as we had arrived just in time to *not* get covered seating by the stage. Instead, we sat one row behind the dry seats while the storm continued. Given that it was Florida, we all assumed the rain would soon pass, but why would things ever turn out well for us?

The rain showed no signs of slowing and, a few minutes into Amy's opening speech, we gave up our various attempts to remain any semblance of dry. Behind us, the rows of the amphitheater slowly emptied, rendering our "priority seating" status all but moot. From the stage, Amy spoke of a concert she attended where it poured rain the entire time. In her case it had united the audience and made them feel like they were a part of something together. Similarly, this Candlelight performance bonded the four of us and we couldn't help but laugh at our soaking wet predicament. When I looked over at Aaron to see how he was holding up, he was shivering but still beaming ear to ear as he watched his lady do her thing.

After the performance, we were in no shape to go anywhere else and so we retreated back to the car. Along the way, I asked Rebekah if she'd like to hang out the next day since Aaron (who was finishing his own book at the time) had to spend most of the afternoon working. She agreed and we made plans for her to pick me up in the morning.

Rebekah arrived sometime before lunch and so we decided to grab some food in the parks. We choose to take a ferryboat over to Magic Kingdom and, before we had even arrived at the MK dock, we had already discussed our mutual affection for *Hairspray,* our hatred of big weddings, and our intentions to elope in order to avoid having big weddings. She even approved of my plan to name my future daughter Aurora Maleficent. As we got our waffle sandwiches from Sleepy Hollow, this level of conversation continued. By the time Aaron arrived to meet us in Hollywood Studios for my first time seeing the Osbourne Family Lights, we had jokingly sketched out our wedding plans.

That evening, as I laid on the air mattress Aaron set up in his living room for me, I texted Rebekah about our New Year's Eve plans. Eventually, I worked up the courage to ask if she might be interested in kissing me at midnight. You could tell that I really meant my question because it lacked the obligatory "lol jk," as was customary even if you were not, indeed, laughing out loud or just kidding... I may have included a winky face though. Unfortunately, she declined my offer, stating that it might be weird since Aaron would be there and I was inclined to agree. In fact, during the rest of the trip I never explicitly told Aaron of my interest in Rebekah. But, since I'm not nearly as cool and coy as I think I am, I'm sure he knew.

After much debate, the three of us decided that the best place for us to spend New Year's would be the Experimental Prototype Community of Tomorrow, otherwise known as Epcot. We had already enjoyed a New Year's Eve Eve celebration in Magic Kingdom the night before as the park ran through all of their festivities (including fireworks and countdown) seemingly as a rehearsal for the "big night." Thus, the choice of which park to ring in the New Year got a little easier.

While our past holiday experiences had prepared us for the crowd levels we would face, it was still surprising to find ourselves waiting 40 minutes for Ellen's Energy Adventure and even being denied a chance to play Agent Perry's World Showcase Adventure. The bulk of the day was spent waiting for the newly reopened Test Track, which I affectionately referred to as "Tron Track." Ironically, I hadn't had a chance to ride the new version yet because the wait time was always too long. On this day, we waited over four hours for the ride... all while listening to the same short music loop. Making the wait even longer was the frequent stops in operation, although, to be fair, that was practically the ride's calling card.

After finally getting to experience Tron Track, we exited into a now-dark Epcot. We decided to make our way around World Showcase and check out the various parties being hosted in some of the pavilions. For example, China held a celebration near its main entrance that I dubbed "The Communist Party." Italy had what was probably the largest party of any pavilion, complete with a DJ and lasers, simulating one of the countries many nightclubs, I assume.

Following our tour around the world, we found ourselves by the Imagination Pavilion. We discovered that Journey Into Imagination with Figment had only a few minute wait and so we decided to ride despite our lack of admiration for the attraction overall. As the safety bar came down, I realized what was about to happen. This was to be our last ride of 2012.

With our disappointing last ride completed, we found a spot near the edge of Mexico to watch Illuminations: Reflections of Earth. We had planned to watch the show and then quickly exit the park in order to make our way over Magic Kingdom, which didn't close until 2 A.M. that night.

Checking our ~~watches~~ phones, we noticed that the show was running a few minutes late. Knowing the usual runtime, we hypothesized that they might pause the show for the countdown to midnight. Unfortunately, this was not the case and, midway through the show, we glanced at our screens, which revealed that midnight had passed. Aaron, Rebekah and I begrudgingly wished each other a happy new year and made our way out of the park. We were on the monorail and ready to depart when the "Countdown to 2013" finally began.

Luckily, I've never been very romantic about New Year's. I never really make resolutions or dream about how this year will be better than the last (to steal a phrase from the Counting Crows). But, despite its botched entry, my year turned out to be the best of my life. Upon my return home, Rebekah and I began dating. Then, in June, we got engaged. Finally, in October and in front of less than a dozen people, we got married. As it turns out, Rebekah doesn't romanticize New Year's very much either. In fact, we spent New Year's Eve 2013 cuddled up in bed where we fell asleep before 10 P.M even rolled around. We reckoned that at least it was past midnight on the East Coast... and even Epcot had to have known it by then.

29
Movie Moment

In order to pull off a great surprise, you need three things: trusted accomplices, a detailed and well-constructed decoy story, and a solid plan of execution. All of these elements take time and shouldn't be rushed, lest the entire plot fall apart before your eyes and ruin whatever surprise you intended to bestow. Yet, somehow, I was able to pull off a Rom-Com-level surprise so masterfully that you'd never believe I dreamt it up in a day.

When Rebekah and I said, "goodbye" in Magic Kingdom in January of 2013, both of us knew something special was brewing. From that point on, we had talked incessantly even as we resided on different coasts, with different time zones, and definitely different sleep schedules. A few weeks into our non-stop textathon, I admitted to her that I had considered running through Fantasyland and down Main Street after her that night. Once I caught up with her, I would give her a grand, spinning camera-style kiss before we split. She then admitted that she kept looking over her shoulder wondering if I would... I guess I had missed my chance at a movie moment.

What's ironic about movies and television is that, for all the glamour and perfection that happens on the screen, the sets and process of shooting them is often quite the opposite. At this point, I had spent the past two years of my life living this dichotomy first hand while working as an extra on dozens of films and television shows. Though sets were often unpredictable, working on them every day — and often on the same show — began adding some normalcy to a very abnormal occupation. Since Rebekah and I were constantly talking throughout the day, she had begun gaining knowledge of the shooting process as well. This would be the first weapon in alibi arsenal.

Fridays were always rough days on a single-camera television show. For many shows, the crew starts with an early call time on Monday (7 A.M. is pretty standard) with the goal of wrapping 12 hours later. Of course, this rarely happens and so you may wrap at 9 P.M. on Monday, which then pushes your start to 9 A.M. on Tuesday. So when you're working on a show with a huge cast that also happens to shoot over 100 music videos in a season as part of their program, Friday night shoots quickly run into Saturday morning.

With another inevitable "Fr-aturday" looming, I sat dressed in my argyle sweater and khakis waiting for myself and the other extras to be called from the nearly empty concrete sound stage we were holding on over to the high school hallway set next door. Once there, we would come to life and pretend to be people ten years younger than our real selves. Of course, we would also pretend it was a bright, sunny morning and not the middle of the night. However, above the padded doors that separated the stages, I could see the red light that signaled "do not enter" flashing on and off meaning that they had already been shooting and didn't need us.

This was also about the time on Friday night when calls would start going out for work on Monday. It was easy to tell when the casting director would start his booking process because, one by one, the most tenured of us extras would reach into our pockets, pull out our phones, and briefly walk away from our lovely metal folding chairs to take the call. Since that hadn't happened yet, I figured it fairly safe to assume that, on Monday, the show would be shooting scenes that were supposed to take place in New

York as opposed to the Ohio high school scenes that I worked.

As much as I was one to never turn down the work when presented with it, I was slightly relieved to have the day off, seeing as it was Rebekah's 27th birthday. At this point, we hadn't even been dating a full month, but deep inside I knew that something special was happening between us. That's when I thought about my missed movie moment and how amazing it would be if I could somehow make it to Orlando to surprise her: surely that would make up for my blown opportunity.

Similar to the story of how I started pricing Tokyo trips "just to see," I grabbed my laptop out of my messenger bag (that doubled as my high school prop) to find out just how expensive a last minute flight to MCO might cost. The first numbers that came in were pretty disheartening. As someone who worked for $64 a day, spending $500 on a three-day trip — including two days where I would possibly have to decline work and, thus, lose more money — seemed impractical at best. Before giving up hope, I tried one last website.

Unfortunately, that site was displaying similar numbers to those I had already seen and dismissed. Then, suddenly, at the top of the list, a red box showed a special fare for nearly $200 cheaper than I had found up until that point. Instead of giving exact departure times or an airline name, the description merely provided me a time frame and said it would have zero to one stops — far better than the two or more stops and still-overly-expensive flights I had found.

Since I had regularly researched Walt Disney World trips in my spare time, I was able to decode this description. I believed that the discount flight being offered to me was a direct flight from LAX to MCO on my favorite domestic airline: Virgin America (that's not a plug, it's just the truth). Even though this all seemed so perfect, spending more than $300 was still probably not the best idea.

Before I had time to pull the trigger, we were finally called to set. I don't remember what scene we were shooting that day since I was far too distracted dreaming about my perfect surprise and how much that was worth to me... monetarily speaking. After more or less convincing myself to do it, I then worried that the deal might be gone by the time we were released from set and sent back to holding. In between takes, I would discreetly take my phone out (this show had a strict no cell phone policy for extras since some fanboys and girls had leaked photos and spoilers from the set in years past) and make sure the flight was still available.

If you're ever on a television set and hear someone yell, "Check the gate!" chances are you will then see a stampede of extras file off of the stage and in the direction of the nearest craft service set up. Instead, those words were my cue to rush back to holding and book my mini-excursion. I refreshed that page, gave the sales page a final once over, and then decided I was missing one important element.

Knowing Rebekah's work schedule, I realized that she was going to have to work at 9 P.M. on Monday. However, she would normally have Tuesdays off, assuming that she didn't switch shifts. The possibility of the latter had me worried along with the fact that I might be crashing someone else plans to surprise her since Reuben or Aaron would definitely be the type to set up an extravagant celebration for her.

With limited time to get this deal done before returning to set, I first called Aaron to see what info he could provide. After telling him my basic plan, he said it all sounded great but that Reuben was planning some birthday dinner for Rebekah and so I better talk to him. Naturally, I called Reuben immediately afterwards.

When I called, Reuben was actually at Rebekah's. I asked him to somehow play off the fact that I was calling and excuse himself from the room. I first asked him if he was planning a dinner for Bekah, to which responded, "Yeah... Did you want to Skype in?" Instead, I asked if I might be able to just come in person, to which he gasped and said, "Yes! That's a much better idea!"

Reuben also confirmed that Bekah did indeed have Tuesday off. This meant that I would at least get to spend one full day with her before returning to LA on Wednesday. That was enough to make the cross-country trip worth it for me, but then, of course, there was the fact that I was going to get to play in Walt Disney World too. With my accomplices in place, I booked my flight.

As I had suspected, my flight was a direct one and on Virgin America. It would also put me in Orlando at around 3 P.M. on Monday, which was just about as perfect as you could get. But, before I got too ahead of myself, I was going to have to flesh out my surprise plans. One of the first people I told about my trip besides Aaron and Reuben was my roommate since she would need to drive me to the airport. This is where my first rookie mistake came in.

While I getting ready to leave my apartment and head to my movie theatre job on Saturday morning, I was on Skype with Rebekah. Before heading out the door, I said goodbye to my roommate who was standing in the kitchen. Not knowing that Bekah was on the phone, she casually said something about taking me to the airport on Monday. Fearful that Bekah has heard, my eyes got large and I began to gesture to change the subject. Then I remembered that I was on Skype and so Bekah could see these gestures, which would surely only heighten her suspension. Luckily, Rebekah didn't mention anything about what she may or may not have just heard long enough for me to come up with a plan. That's when I decided that my story would be that I had been booked to work on Monday and that we were filming on location at the Van Nuys Airport.

The key to having a believable story is to think about all of the possible details first so that, when asked, you can provide them quickly and convincingly. However, if you divulge all of these details without prompting, it begins to raise eyebrows and you could well be made. That's why, instead of panicking once this airport blunder occurred, I went on with normal conversation and only told Rebekah later in the day that I had been booked for Monday. That way, when I told her it was to be on location in Van Nuys and she came back with, "But I thought I heard 'airport,' " I could say, "Yeah, the Van Nuys Airport." — never would I ever mention the word "airport" unless she mentioned it first. Luckily, she never did.

With my end of the — well, let's just call it what it is — *lie* in place, it was time to secure things on the eastern end. Reuben and Aaron made plans to meet Rebekah at Magic Kingdom at about the time I would be arriving. Unfortunately, this is normally about when Bekah would like to be napping prior to her overnight shift. To keep her from backing out, Reuben told Rebekah that it was Aaron who had a surprise for her. Later on, Reuben would then update her saying that Aaron had pre-purchased dinner for the three of them at Tony's on Main Street and made it seem like *that* was the surprise. It. Was. Brilliant.

We also devised the perfect place for us to meet: the porch behind Sleepy Hollow in Liberty Square. Back when I had visited in December, Bekah and I had our first date (that we didn't know was a date at the time) at the restaurant and we had talked about how great it would be if the building attached to that nearby porch was our home. Since that specific structure did have some significance, it was going to be a little tricky telling her to meet them there without any red flags going up. This is where I truly began impressing even myself.

My logic, as I presented it to my co-conspirators, was that Aaron, being the Starbucks-fiend that he is, would want coffee upon entering the parks. Since coffee is something that Sleepy Hollow offered, this was a reasonable alibi. However, you can never be too careful with such things, so I added some back-up details just in case.

Reuben was to going to be working in Fantasyland just before our meet up time and so I figured that Liberty Square would be a good, central meeting location. Not to mention that there was a utilidor access point nearby, making this lie the best it could possibly be. Ultimately, it wasn't until after I had surprised Rebekah that I told her all of the details I had thought out. Instead, she just accepted this meeting spot without thinking twice about it.

When Monday came, I got up at 5 A.M. to secretly travel to LAX. I had told Rebekah that my call time was 6 A.M. and so this also fit into my fictional timeline. Plus, had I actually been working, a six o'clock call would put our lunchtime at noon Pacific, which is about the time I would land at MCO. Bekah was still awake after having worked until 5 A.M. and so we had a few minutes for me to complain to her about how much I hated location shoots and, of course, wish her a happy birthday.

Since she might find it odd that I didn't talk to her for the five hours it would take me to fly to Orlando, I also told her that we'd most likely be on set the majority of the day and so I wouldn't be able to text much thanks to that "no cell phones on set" policy. When I landed, I told her we had just gotten a short break, but that crew call was actually in at 7 A.M., meaning lunch wouldn't be for another hour.

Aaron picked me up from the airport a few short hours later and we headed straight to Magic Kingdom. Thanks to traffic, our drive there took more time than we expected; the first wrinkle in our plan. When we finally hit Disney property (nearly 20 minutes late), we decided to try parking at the Contemporary Resort to save time and get back on schedule. Unfortunately, we were turned away since we didn't have confirmed reservations (or reservations at all… but they didn't need to know that).

As we made our U-turn to head out, Aaron thought he had spotted Re-bekah over on the nearby sidewalk. Before he looked closer to confirm it was her, I ducked down as far as I could, lest my surprise be ruined after having come so far literally and figuratively. A later inquiry confirmed that she had indeed parked at the Contemporary and was also running late, making it very likely that it was her on that sidewalk. Still, we had narrowly avoided disaster.

We eventually parked elsewhere and made our way into the parks. As I walked down Main Street, I was still texting Bekah about my day on set. According to my story, we had taken a penalty on lunch (meaning they would pay us a bonus to delay the meal and finish the shot they were on) but would be breaking soon.

Before we got to the restaurant, Aaron decided to let me go alone and have my movie moment. As I approached the porch, I could see Rebekah sitting there, still texting me back thinking I was in Van Nuys, California instead of 10 feet from her. I stood right in front of her and simply said, "Hey." She looked up and after a second of confusion and/or disbelief, she hugged me hard and shook a little almost as though she was frightened. When I could get the words out in between fits of laughter, I said, "Happy birthday," to which she just kept saying, "You're here!"

When she was finally able to look at me, her face was bright red and she had an awful lot of questions. Paramount amongst her other queries was how long I was going to be in town for. I told her I would be there until Wednesday (incidentally, the day *before* Valentine's Day) and so we could spend all of Tuesday together. Predictably, her next question was, "Do I really have to go to work tonight?!"

We met up with Aaron and Reuben in Fantasyland a few minutes later. Once there, we confessed to all of our lies over the past weekend. After confirming it was worth it, both of my partners in crime went off to work before rejoining us later in the night.

My movie moment was a rousing success, but now it had ended. Part of that trip back down to earth included the realization that I had spent hundreds of dollars that I probably shouldn't have. Being as sweet as she is, Bekah picked up on this and decided she'd buy dinner even though it was her birthday.

If the rest of this story makes me sound like the best boyfriend ever, the fact that I let my girlfriend pay for her birthday dinner and that said dinner consisted of kids meals at Captain Cook's probably levels me out on the boyfriend ranking chart. Before we headed out of the park, we stopped on the Tomorrowland bridge in the shadow of Cinderella Castle and we shared our first kiss together. Little did we know that it would end up being the last first kiss for each of us.

30
Sanaa

I've never been an adventurous eater. In fact, my diet has most accurately been compared to that of a five year old. I order my cheeseburgers with only meat and cheese on them, eat few fruits or vegetables, and react to finding a mushroom in my food the way someone might if they had found a cockroach instead. So what would lead me to eat at an Indian/African fusion restaurant in Animal Kingdom Lodge?

While I was in Florida surprising my girlfriend, Rebekah, for her birthday, she mentioned that her friends had planned to take us to lunch and for a round of putt-putt golf the next day. In the morning, I got a text with more detailed plans stating that we would be going to "sanaa." The lack of punctuation in the text led me to believe that, perhaps, "sanaa" was short hand for something I was unaware of. After all, Disney fans had made such acronyms as HISTA (Honey, I Shrunk the Audience), CoP (Carousel of Progress), and the initialism of Monsters Inc. Laugh Floor commonplace.

My first thought was that maybe it was an abbreviation for one of the mini-golf courses. I had never been to either and so their titles had temporarily escaped me. Without explaining, I asked Aaron for the names of the course. Unfortunately, Fantasia Gardens nor Winter Summerland provided the letters I needed to fill out the mysterious word. Next my thought was that it might be a resort. Running through a mental list, I again enlisted Aaron in my efforts.

Eventually, Aaron put an end to these charades and bluntly questioned why I was asking such questions. I showed him the text and asked, "What is this?" He laughed and informed me that it wasn't an acronym, but a restaurant pronounced "suh-nah." Although he had never eaten there, he said that everyone he knew that had not only raved about it but also proceeded to never shut up about it. This was quickly followed up with, "But I have no idea what *you* would have to eat there."

The next logical step was to look up the menu online. Unfortunately, the entree menu wasn't very detailed. Butter chicken and beef short ribs sounded great, but I figured there'd inevitably be some ingredient that would ruin the dish for me. Frustratingly, I just didn't know what it would be yet. Adding to this dining anxiety, assuming I did find a dish that suited me, it would set me back over $20.

After a round of putt-putt at Winter Summerland (where we choose to play the "summer" side), it was time for lunch. It wasn't until we were walking into the place that I informed Rebekah that I was prepared to resign to eating only naan bread. My logic was that I didn't want to tell her earlier, have everyone scramble to accommodate me, and end up being disappointed.

Our table was located right next to the large windows that exposed the vast landscape outside which was also inhabited by wildlife. Well, I'm not sure how wild wildlife can be when they reside at a hotel, but still. At this point, I felt a little bit better about the experience because at least if I did eat only bread for lunch, I could stare at a giraffe while I did it.

The printed menus at the restaurant were as vague as those found online, but was supplemented some by our waiter's explanations of what we could expect. Deciding that if I was brave enough to spend two weeks in Tokyo by myself, I should be brave enough to have lunch at a Walt Disney World Resort restaurant, I ponied up and ordered the aforementioned butter chicken and beef short ribs. Luckily, this combo was served with basmati, so now my meal had been upgraded to at least bread and rice.

When the food came, it was served in three small bowls: one contained a sauce and a piece of chicken, one with a different sauce and some beef, and another with the rice. At this point, I realized I had probably overreacted. Additionally, the lack of descriptors on the menu wasn't some cunning trick to hide ingredients from picky eaters like myself, but a simple reflection of the lack of ingredients in the dish.

To my surprise, the food was actually quite tasty. After devouring it all, I even found myself hungry for more. Rebekah looked down at my empty dishes and then up to me as if to say, "See? And you were scared." Of course, the tameness of the food didn't stop me from acting like I had eaten a barbecued rattlesnake or fried monkey brain. I even tweeted a photo of the menu, making sure everyone could see the tagline "The Art of African Cooking with Indian Flavors" was clearly visible. When I returned to Aaron's place, I started to tell him my tale.

"You would be so proud of me. You'll never guess what I ate for lunch…"

31
The Big Reveal

They say turn-about is fair play and so it seemed only logical that Rebekah could get her revenge on the friends who had withheld a major secret from her only a few months earlier. After my surprise birthday visit in February of 2013, it became increasingly clear to both Rebekah and me that the relationship we were in was to be unlike any other either of us had previously experienced. Complicating the matter was the fact that we were still living on opposite coasts.

March of that year marked my third straight month of traveling to Walt Disney World from Los Angeles. This trip promised to be a little different because, instead of staying on an air mattress in Aaron's living room, I would be staying at a timeshare in Bonnet Creek (a small area of land surrounded by Walt Disney World property) owned by Bekah's parents. Incidentally, the timeshare reservation hadn't actually been made for us but for Bekah's younger brother and his college friends who had chosen Orlando as their spring break destination.

Somehow I still wound up sleeping in the living room, as Rebekah and I got the pull out sofa for ourselves. This way we could be together but in a public enough setting lest anyone assume any hanky and/or panky was taking place. Between that and sticking ourselves on cooking duties for the quartet of collegiate co-eds, Rebekah and I seemed to be acting more and more like a married couple. Because of this, it seemed only natural when, upon my return back to the Pacific, we began discussing the steps towards making that a reality.

With such matters, timing is everything. However, more often than not, practicality plays a big part in the decision process as well. The reality was that Rebekah's apartment lease would be up in September, meaning that she'd either have to move out then or re-sign and stay for another year. Even though both of us found all warnings against long-distance relationships wrought with exaggeration, the thought of spending a minimum of 18 months living a five-hour flight away from each other was not an appealing option by any means.

This isn't to say that the constraints placed on our relationship weren't without their silver linings. Perhaps it would have been a different story if we had already grown accustomed to spending as much time as we wanted together while living in the same city before one of us departed for one reason or another. However, since our love was distanced from the beginning, it seemed easier to just accept and make the best of it.

Since the set up of our relationship rarely allowed us to go to movies, dinners, or enjoy other distractions, Rebekah and I had spent nearly every available minute we had simply conversing… for hours… for months. Consequently, even though we had only been dating for a few short weeks, I knew more than enough about her to convince me that she fulfilled each and every one of my long list of requirements for wifely contention. As they say, "When you know, you know."

Having made three trips east, May marked Rebekah's turn to come visit me in Los Angeles. By this time, we might as well have just called ourselves engaged since we had already laid out a plan to marry and move in together. Because the actual proposal would be little more than formality and we both agreed to have a small, simple wedding, I had planned on arranging an elaborate and creative proposal worthy of viral video status.

After looking into various flash mobs for hire, I later set my sights a little closer to earth. That's when I figured, what better place than Disneyland would there be make a magical memory with my (hopeful) bride-to-be? At this point Bekah had never even been to the original Magic Kingdom, and so the only park where Walt walked seemed ripe with opportunity for such a tremendous event.

Alas, there was one big problem with this plan: Rebekah had made it clear that she would like for me to ask her father (er, parents, but more on that later) for his blessing before we made our engagement official. Further complicating the matter was the fact that I had yet to meet her parents (or her mine, for that matter). I guess in a whirlwind things are bound to get a little messed up.

Rebekah's May trip quickly came and went. Unfortunately, she returned to Orlando without any new jewelry to display. In June, I once again hopped on a plane, but this time MCO was not my destination, but, instead, I would be traveling to the oh-so-exciting town of Cleveland, Ohio. Adding insult to injury, Virgin America doesn't fly to Cleveland because, well, why would they?

My reasons for visiting the Midwest on this occasion sound like the premise of a romantic comedy. In fact, I'm pretty sure Ben Stiller and Robert Di Niro already made it. First, Rebekah's younger brother (not that one, a different one) was getting married. I was invited to join as Bekah's plus one at what can only be considered the last minute by wedding standards. Secondly, not only would this be my first chance to meet Bekah's parents, but I would also be staying at their house for the entire week I was in town.

The day after the wedding — having known Rebekah's parents for all of three days or so — the four of us went to lunch. Towards the end of the meal, Rebekah and I began setting the stage for what would eventually (a key word in this tale) end in our engagement. As I began to explain how I felt about their daughter, Bekah's mom stopped me and insisted we should wait until we got home. I complied and we awkwardly paid our check and headed back to the house.

After offering a round of beverages, Rebekah's mother joined us on the family's porch, armed with a pen and a legal pad of paper. This is when the long day of questioning began. Imagine a deposition mixed with an interview of a presidential candidate and that's probably in the ballpark of what transpired.

Literal hours later, our conversation was again interrupted as the rest of the family demanded dinner be prepared. Yes, it had been that long and it didn't stop there. Following the second meal of the interrogation, we resumed our chat about whether or not I use foul language and whether I found Wishes or Remember... Dreams Come True to be the superior fireworks show — or something like that.

Around the eight-hour mark, Bekah's father offered his blessing. Her mother, however, seemed as if she still had another few hours of questioning before she was actually ready to sign off on the deal. By this time, it was nearly 10 P.M., leaving me little time for a clever proposal.

Instead, I took Rebekah into the room I had been staying in, played a song from my iPhone (Peter Gabriel's gorgeous cover of The Magnetic Fields' "The Book of Love") and we danced together. At the song's conclusion, I presented her with a hollowed out book that was covered with images of various worldly destinations. Inside of it hung a small amethyst ring on a chain — the stone representing the month of her birth and the chain because her profession in culinary disallowed hand jewelry. This is when I got down on my knee and said four words I wondered if I'd ever get to utter myself: "Will you marry me?"

Immediately after she accepted my proposal, we went downstairs to officially inform the rest of her family of the news. Soon after, I called my parents as well. However, our announcement came with a rather odd embargo: we asked that no one post congratulations on our Facebooks or other social media profiles until we gave the go-ahead. We had multiple reasons for this, the first being that we didn't want to "steal the thunder" of Rebekah's sibling who had barely just left for his honeymoon. Secondly, Rebekah wanted to inform our friends who were there for our first meeting, Aaron and Reuben, of the news in person.

Thanks to busy schedules amongst the three of them, it would be at least a week before Bekah, Aaron, and Reuben could all meet. Meanwhile, during my near-daily conversations with Aaron, it was growing increasingly difficult to not share what was to be the single most important event in my life. Finally, the trio made plans to have brunch on a Saturday morning in Downtown Disney.

At the same time Rebekah was in Walt Disney World, about to drop the proverbial bombshell on our friends, I was stuck in the lobby of a multiplex, watching the trickle of customers that see films that early in the morning purchase their popcorn and head to their auditoriums. Discreetly, I would sneak away to the arcade area of the theatre, take out my cell phone, and attempt to cover it with my suit jacket. I hotly anticipated that my phone would blow-up with reaction once the boys found out the news.

The way Rebekah told them had actually been planned back when I was still in Cleveland at her parent's house. In Aaron's book, *The Thinking Fan's Guide to Walt Disney World: Magic Kingdom,* Rebekah is credited in the acknowledgements as an "in-park research assistant." We then came up with the idea for her to write a letter of resignation from this position, given her impending relocation to California. Just in case that wasn't clear enough, she then mentioned that any further credits should be done using what was to be her new name: Rebekah Burbank.

When Bekah handed Aaron the letter at the conclusion of their meal at Wolfgang Puck Express, he didn't know what to make of it. At first he thought that maybe she had gotten in trouble at work for her involvement in an unauthorized Disney book. Then, he figured out that she was moving. Still, that last detail eluded him until Reuben noticed the amethyst ring dangling from Bekah's neck.

"Shut the front door!" Reuben yelled, just as we had predicted he would. As I checked my phone for the thousandth consecutive minute, my screen finally illuminated with congratulations in the form of caps and exclamation marks. Later that day, the social media embargo was lifted and we informed the world of our impending nuptials.

By this point, it was nearly July. Rebekah would meet both of my parents in September and then we would wed in October. At that point, our courtship would barely reach nine months in age. When you inform people of such a timeline, they assume a baby must be on the way. For us there were no children yet — just two kids who found their perfect love.

32
Send-Off

Before Rebekah and I got married, I took one last trip to Florida to help her pack up and travel back west to California by car. Of course, I had to make one more trip to Walt Disney World as well. The last Disney park I set foot in as a single man was my favorite of the four Florida parks: Epcot.

Prior to heading over for our last night in World Showcase, my fiancé and I visited Disney's Animal Kingdom with our friend Reuben, as DAK was the one park that Rebekah and I hadn't kissed in yet. This can be attributed to the fact that we rarely went there on account of it being my least favorite. Ironically, Animal Kingdom is actually the park where we met.

A year and a half prior, while Aaron and I were enjoying the rarity of "DAK in the dark" (pronounced with a Bostonian accent), we stopped off near the exit to Dinosaur so we could meet up with two of Aaron's friends who were in line for the ride. Before we had even shaken hands, Reuben approached me and said, "Kyle Burbank! I've seen you on TV!"

I laughed, as I wasn't *really* on TV and he wouldn't actually have noticed me if Aaron hadn't paused his TiVo (which I made him name Tim — Tim TiVo) to point me out in a crowded hallway.

His other friend was Rebekah. Unlike Reuben, she was unfamiliar with my "work" as a colorful blur on *Glee* but was impressed nevertheless. The four of us then chatted about life in Los Angeles while stopping off for some darjeeling tea at one of the park's quick service kiosks. Inevitably, the conversation led back to my role as an extra and one scene in particular where I helped one of the main characters, Mr. Schuester, propose by handing his girlfriend a rose as they walked down the hallway. Rebekah remembered the scene but not necessarily my part in it.

Later that night, she went home and re-watched the scene in question only to see my dumb, half-smiling face staring back at her (an expression that my friends had dubbed "The Proud Parent"). She then remembered that, at the time of its original airing, she questioned why random nerds they had never seen before on the series were involved in such an important moment in the show's story.

Growing up, Rebekah had always dreamed about the type of man she might one day marry. It was her seemingly naive belief that when she saw the one for her, there would be music. Years later, via television and the nature of *Glee*, the first time she saw me there was literally music. To be sure, it was not anything classically romantic — a Rihanna song that may or may not be about Chris Brown — but the point is that there was music. While Rihanna found love in a hopeless place, we had found love in the Happiest Place on Earth.

Flash forward to our last night in Florida, Rebekah and I wandered to the spot where we had met 18 months prior. Reuben snapped a photo of us and immediately posted it to Facebook, proud of the meaningful moment he had captured and his role in our romantic plot. After our brief excursion, we headed over to Epcot to meet Aaron for dinner.

With little discussion necessary, we selected Teppan Edo as the site for our send-off meal. The week that I met Rebekah, Aaron and I had invited her to join us for our first time dining at the Japan Pavilion. However, she was forced to cancel when another friend needed her assistance. Because of that lunch-that-never-was and the fact that we planned to visit Tokyo for our honeymoon, it seemed like it would be the perfect place to celebrate together. We debated how cheesy to make our last dinner together, briefly considering a plan to have each of us purchase chopsticks from the pavilion shop to use for the meal and keep afterwards as a souvenir. Instead, we figured our memories would suffice, although a couple of photos couldn't hurt.

The food was even better than I remembered and our chef impressed us with both her skills and her humor. When we told her that I was from California, she asked if I had ever heard the term "hella good." She explained that she had a friend in Northern California she had visited who used the term incessantly. I told her I had, indeed, heard the term and she then continued to use it for the rest of the evening. "This is the yum yum sauce — it's hella good." Unbeknownst to her, this may not have realized that this might not have been 100 percent Disney appropriate, but no one else at our table seemed to mind.

Teppan Edo's seating arrangement puts you in a position (literally) to interact with the other guests at your table. Each hibachi seats eight guests so there's a good chance you'll be seated with people you don't know. When the other guests discovered the significance of our meal, a standard round of "Awwwww" was released. Then when our waitress served our dessert — green tea and vanilla swirled ice cream — she included an origami heart on which she wrote "happily ever after" in Japanese symbols. Upon its presentation and explanation, the table engaged in an encore round of "Awwww."

After dinner, Aaron gifted Rebekah and me with a statuette of Mickey and Minnie in a tuxedo and wedding dress, respectively. In the parking lot of the Boardwalk Resort, where Rebekah had worked for the past four years, we said our goodbyes and headed home to prepare for the long trek ahead. Only a few hours later, we awoke and began attempting to fit all of Rebekah's life into her compact Ford Focus. Somehow we managed, save half a dozen boxes or so that Reuben graciously offered to ship to us. We left Orlando that morning and were up to the Florida Panhandle by sunrise, determined to make it to Houston before calling it a day. The car was so full that Aaron's gift sat in the passenger's lap the entire way. Often we'd look down at it remembering the journey we'd taken to that point and looking forward to the one we'd be taking together for the rest of our lives.

33
Celeste

For my friends and I, Disneyland is where we go for almost any occasion. We go there to celebrate, to hang out together, or just go alone to write. We take new friends, old friends, crushes, and beaus there to show them what we love so much about the park and hope they appreciate them as much as we do. The problem with this is that not every relationship with every person we bring to Disneyland is going to have that classic Disney happy ending. When such relationships do turn sour, the memories you've made in the park together can be sullied as well.

My friend, whom we'll call Kristoff, met a girl we'll call Celeste when they dined together at Club 33. I had known Celeste from work and we had actually bonded over our love of Disney. She once told me that she used to jog while listening to the Remember... Dreams Come True soundtrack and I was instantly smitten. It was a similar story for Kristoff, who met her while dining with a group of friends and made sure to get her number before they parted.

At the time, Celeste was just a friend of mine. A few months later, we briefly had what some outsiders or myself might call a romantic relationship. Celeste didn't see it this way. Of course, the fact that she wanted it to remain a secret should have been a bright red flag. Once I sobered up to the real nature of our relationship, I attempted to keep my distance. We still worked together and had several mutual friends, so I put on my game face until the anger and hurt subsided.

Around the time that I was turning the page on this fling, Kristoff and few of our other friends decided it was time for my first visit to Goofy's Kitchen in the Disneyland Hotel. Kristoff invited Celeste, as I had kept my vow of silence and had not spoken of how our friendship had changed. While I was, for all intents and purposes, over Celeste, I still had a sinking feeling in my stomach the whole night (not a great thing to have at a buffet) as nightmare scenarios played through my head about all the different things that could go wrong with one offhand remark.

Kristoff and Celeste were thick as thieves that evening, somewhat to the chagrin of the rest of our party. Celeste has a strong personality (to put it delicately), which proved too much for one of our guests who was meeting her for the first time. As we left the restaurant and headed to Trader Sam's, I took some joy in watching the unhappy camper roll her eyes and snark quietly to herself about Celeste's behavior. If she only knew...

By the time we took our places for World of Color, everyone except Kristoff and Celeste seemed about ready to call it a night. Luckily, we did so right after the show. As I arrived home, the texts started to pour in asking why my behavior was off that evening. I chalked it up to nerves but claimed I didn't know what had caused them.

A few months later, Kristoff needed a place to stay and so he had moved into Celeste's condo. The plan was for the two of them to have a short trial as roommates and, if it went well, they could move to a less expensive apartment once they found one. By this time, I had met the woman who would go on to be my wife and was far removed from my Celeste episode. Because of this, I had no objection to their arrangement and was even somewhat happy for the two of them.

The trial period seemed to go well and the two started looking for a place... until it suddenly fell apart. As it turned out, Kristoff and Celeste briefly had what some outsiders, myself, or Kristoff might call a romantic relationship. Celeste didn't see it this way.

This fallout hit Kristoff harder than it did when it happened to me. He had never really found the perfect girl but thought he had in Celeste. She was pretty, silly, and loved Disney — that's the dream. On top of that, they had met at Club 33, of all places. How could it get any more magical?

When Kristoff was ready to talk, another friend and I took him out to Disneyland. There, for the first time, I revealed my own experience with Celeste. As Kristoff and I compared notes, the pieces all fell into place. Not only had Celeste done essentially the same thing to each of us, it seemed that she was also trying to turn us against each other.

Even after hearing all the lies Celeste had told to each of us, Kristoff still missed her. He talked about how part of the parks were now ruined for him: World of Color since we had watched it after dinner that night, Aladdin since they had their first kiss after singing "Whole New World," and Fantasmic just because of how much she loved it. While it wouldn't be easy, we knew what we had to do.

From that day forward, we worked to reclaim those Disneyland memories for Kristoff by replacing them with new and happy ones. Our friendship not only survived Hurricane Celeste, it grew stronger, despite her best efforts. We still don't dare speak her name between each other (Voldemort or "She Who Must Not Be Named" are common replacements), but he has, for the most part, moved on. And so, while his story with Celeste didn't have that classic Disney happy ending, his affair with Disneyland continues towards that famed happily ever after.

T·O·K·Y·O

34
The One Where
I Went Back to Tokyo

The second time I visited Tokyo was four years to the day that I arrived the first time. In those four years, a vast number of things had changed in my life and, some would say, I had grown up a lot. On my first visit, I was in my early twenties, single, and came alone on vacation to explore. Four years later, I was in my late twenties, married, and visiting as a delayed honeymoon with my wife, Rebekah.

I've never felt as old as I am— at least not after my teen years — nor have I known exactly how to "act" my age. I'd often joke that I was the age the characters were in season five of *Friends* and how impossibly strange that seemed to me. Coincidentally, as I searched through the entertainment offerings of Singapore Airlines on our way to Narita Airport in 2014, I found that they were featuring a dozen or so episodes from that very season. Naturally, I watched nearly all of them during the 11-hour flight.

Since we spent next to nothing on our wedding, my wife and I always had the plan of spending whatever gifts we received from our nuptials on a nice honeymoon. This, of course, meant that we couldn't go straight from our wedding venue to our chosen destination like most couples do. Instead, we collected the checks that rolled into our mailbox over the few weeks following our vows until we could book our vacation.

When I had first suggested going to Tokyo for our honeymoon, Rebekah agreed almost immediately. At the time, we were still living on opposite coasts and having what we called "Skype Movie Dates Nights." This would consist of us booting up Skype to talk, streaming movies on Netflix, and then playing them simultaneously. Since Rebekah had never seen *Lost In Translation*, I insisted we watch it "together" so she could see what I loved so much about the film and the city itself.

As much as I wanted to explore the vast city of Tokyo with Bekah and experience some of the things that I missed on my first trip, I'd be lying if I didn't say that taking her to Tokyo DisneySea was my top priority. Knowing her infatuation with Epcot and what was in store for her in the park convinced me that DisneySea would surpass the Florida's second gate to become her favorite Disney Park by the time we left. Plus, by this point, my itch to return to the extravagant resort was growing nearly unbearable.

After we got engaged, I again attempted to learn some Japanese before our trip. For the first month, I was very good about completing my recommended half-hour a day class. Now I could not only say "good morning," "good evening," and "thank you" but could also tell you that the dog is blue or that I'd like to order some green tea. Naturally this attempt at being bilingual fell apart quickly and I, once again, said little more than "thank you" in Japanese on this second excursion.

Once we had the money in place, it was time to select the dates for our late-honeymoon. As I mentioned, we actually ended up choosing the exact same dates as when I had ventured east (well, actually west from California) the first time. Furthermore, we decided to stay at the same hotel not only because of my positive prior experience there but also (and more importantly) because the price was right. Plus, the added bonus of knowing where I was going was attractive since I had failed at making any headway on the language front.

When we booked our visit, it was still over 100 days away. I know this because we had a countdown on our phones that we would frequently turn to for updates as the time grew near. As our countdown hit the single digits, it was time for us to purchase some yen (side note: it can be a bit intimidating to walk into a small shop in Van Nuys and ask for 30,000 of anything, even it if that did only convert to around $300), dust off the larger luggage, and suffer through the last few days of work before I would return to the land of the rising sun.

Even before we set off for the airport, things were coming up Milhouse... er, Burbank. As I went to check us in for our flight, I noticed that I was able to move our seats to the second level (yes, this plane had an upstairs) for no charge. In addition to the novelty of riding on the upper deck of a plane, the rows on each side of the second level economy section had only two seats each as opposed to typical three. This meant that my wife and I could have a window and an aisle without having some pesky stranger separating us.

During the flight, my wife tried to sleep in between watching some of the movies that were offered while I enjoyed that aforementioned *Friends* marathon. Even though I had seen those episodes dozens of times, I always laugh at almost every punch line regardless. The familiarity of the show and likeability of its characters makes watching it an experience I'm always excited to return to. Yet, I still feel all the same emotions I did the first time I watched and even find myself feeling anxious for the friends when things don't go quite to plan. This is what visiting Tokyo for the second time was like as well.

When we landed in Japan, everything suddenly came rushing back to me as though I had never left. Even though navigating to the hotel was a much less daunting ordeal this time around, the language barrier still reared its ugly head and I continued to make mistakes such as my silly American brain forgetting to walk up on the left side of the staircase. Still, seeing the look on my wife's face as we took in the beautiful details of the city made it clear we had chosen the right place for our honeymoon.

Just as I had done on my initial visit, we spent the first few days of the trip exploring various parts of the city. The bus tickets we had purchased to take us from Narita Airport into the heart of Tokyo also came with a two-day unlimited ticket for the subway, which we made good use of. With few actual goals in mind, my wife and I exited the train at random parts and just walked around.

One of the first things my wife noticed about Tokyo was just how happy the majority of the people there seemed to be. She was shocked to see how friendly everyone we encountered was and how they seemed to bend over backwards in order to communicate with the dumb foreigners who couldn't keep up with their Rosetta Stone lessons. Rebekah also seemed to enjoy all the same activities I did during my solo-trip: walking, going to record stores, and remarking on how unique and interesting much of the architecture in the city was.

The only thing we didn't agree on was the food. While Rebekah was game to get a little adventurous with our dining, I remained terrified of visiting most establishments for many reasons. For one, I was still extremely intimidated by engaging in conversation with someone I couldn't understand. Secondly, considering that I usually request to remove at least one item from any dish I order in America, having no idea what was going to be served on my food in Japan worried me greatly. As much as I pleaded with Rebekah to just go wherever she wanted to go, she refused and I subjected the poor girl to American fast food for the bulk of our honeymoon. We even ordered Dominos (which is delivered via a driver on a small scooter) into our room. Twice.

With my luck, the one food item in Tokyo I was overjoyed to experience once again was nowhere to be found. On my first visit, there was a shop in Shibuya that occupied the corner of one the many small alleys that make up the district. There they sold amazing creations known as taiyaki. Imagine a waffle shaped like a fish stuffed with your choice of fillings ranging from chocolate to cheeseburger. My favorite was the "Germany Potato" that contained mashed potatoes and bacon. Plus, the servers all wore fish-shaped hats on their head; it was as delicious as it was delightfully Japanese. Unfortunately, after multiple false alarms and several circular trips around the area, I had to conclude that my beloved taiyaki stand was no more.

Still a little bummed about my snack seemingly swimming away from me, I talked Rebekah into visiting the Tokyo Disneyland resort in the evening as a "preview day." As part of the deal, I said we could find the walking route to each of the parks from Maihama Station so that we could avoid paying for the resort monorail this time around. This part of the preview day took all of five minutes, as the path to Tokyo Disneyland could not have been easier to find.

After staving off the temptation to buy any extra day in the park, we instead decided to explore the Disneyland Hotel that sits right across from the main gates. Since I had been so concerned about spending time in the parks in 2010, I never took to the time to check out the resort's three hotels. Following our short look around the first one, we made our way towards Tokyo DisneySea, stopping at the Disney Ambassador Hotel on the way.

To be honest, I didn't even know of the Ambassador's existence until that moment. We really only stumbled upon it because the pond, bridge, and gazebo that sit to the side of the hotel caught our eyes. The art-deco design of the resort felt immediately Disney and in the vein of California Adventure (2.0) and Hollywood Studios. In fact, upon entering it became apparent that Hollywood was a large part of the hotel's theming. It was a strange experience to travel half way around the world only to walk into a hotel themed to your hometown.

The next step on our journey was Tokyo DisneySea and the Hotel MiraCosta. From the window just past the lobby of the MiraCosta, we could see into the gorgeous DisneySea. Immediately I began pointing out a number of the attractions to my wife: "See Tower over there?" "This is the bay where Fantasmic plays," "Watch, there's going to be a car that shoots out of that volcano." As difficult as declining an extra day in Tokyo Disneyland was, doing the same for DisneySea was dang near impossible.

Before my heart could overpower my head (and wallet), we headed back towards Ikspiari — a shopping area that could be called Tokyo Disneyland's equivalent of Downtown Disney where we ate some dinner and looked in the various gift shops. One of the strangest things to me was that Ikspiari not only had Disney Parks-style gift shops but also a Disney Store that offered different merchandise. Prior to heading back to the hotel, we decided to purchase our four-day tickets to save time on our park day.

The next morning, we arrived to the gates of Disneyland 30 minutes before park opening. To my somewhat surprise, the area was mobbed with various long lines. These lines were so long that it was hard to get a good enough view to determine whether they lead to the gates of the park or to the ticket counters. Eventually, we decided just to get in line and see what happened.

Luckily, we were in the right line, but our plan of getting straight over to Monsters Inc. Ride and Go Seek was sullied (pun intended). Plan 'B' became to get a FastPass and return later, however, the line to get a FastPass was enormous and growing by the second. Fearing it would sell out, we bit the bullet and joined the three-hour line. I apologized profusely to my wife and offered to try again later, but made it clear that I was going to ride the attraction one way or another this time.

Though the wait was still longer than I would have liked, it wasn't actually three hours. Besides, once we made it to the interior portion of the queue there were enough dorky details to entertain me. Walking in to that area legitimately felt like I was walking into the Monsters Inc. building. It was simultaneously the same and completely opposite of walking into Carsland. In one I was stepping into my favorite Pixar film and the other I was stepping into my least favorite Pixar film.

The attraction was worth both the four-year wait to return to it as well as the two-plus hours to ride it. However, as we exited we began to notice that it was not only that ride commanding a long wait. I was a bit perplexed considering there were nearly no crowds at the same date four years prior, but there was one fatal flaw in my plan: this time we were attending on a Sunday instead of a weekday.

To make the best of our mistake, we tried our hardest to utilize FastPasses and visit attractions that might not be as popular — like The Country Bears or The Tiki Room. Still, it was becoming clear that Bekah wasn't overly impressed with our visit. At a certain point, we decided it may just be best to call it a night so that we could arrive earlier for our DisneySea visit the next day.

From the time the doors on our Maihama-bound train closed at Tokyo Station, it was evident that the crowds would be much lighter at the resort that day. When we finished our long trek to the front gates, there were only a dozen or so guests in each turnstile line. Once the park opened, we took the opportunity to grab Tower of Terror FastPasses before I took Rebekah on a mandatory, preliminary tour of the park.

Within minutes, it was obvious that she was falling in love. I could see her excitement grow with every step we took. By the time we got back around to Mysterious Island, she hardly believed me when I said, "Now for the best part." And yet I was right.

We spent the entire day in the park, even staying to watch Fantasmic that evening. As we walked back to the train, Rebekah had hinted that Epcot might have just been dethroned. There was also no question where we would be spending our first park hopper day.

Though we started in DisneySea the next morning, we eventually migrated over to Land to finish up the attractions we had missed due to crowds and to experience the DreamLights parade. I thought I had kept pretty good tabs on the park in my absence, but the news of Tokyo's version of Disney's Electrical Parade gaining some new floats apparently eluded me. Other than that, not too much else about the park had changed.

For our final day — the resorts 31st birthday — we still had one thing left to do in Tokyo Disneyland. Up until that point, Rebekah and I had photos of us in front of Sleeping Beauty Castle in Disneyland and Cinderella Castle in Walt Disney World. While we were dating, those photos perfectly illustrated our bi-costal relationship. Now it was time to add a third photograph to that collection; one that would signify our new life together and all the experiences we would come to share.

With our third castle conquered, we returned to DisneySea to soak in the beauty once more. The day was punctuated with people watching sessions and multiple rides of Sindbad's Storybook Voyage — a personal favorite. Per Rebekah's request, we again stayed to watch Fantasmic together before taking a final nighttime stroll around the park prior to close.

The last few days of our trip following our Disney visit went quickly and were spent much the same way we had spent the first couple with some exceptions. One of the days we ventured to an aquarium and visited a tower's observation deck where, it just so happened, my friend Arielle's photography from her book *365 Days of Danboard* was being displayed. We also finally got to visit the Studio Ghibli museum that I had so foolishly passed up before. This was also when we were first introduced to Tsum Tsums, which would make their American debut a few months afterwards.

Leaving Tokyo the second time was even harder than the first. While I was very much ready to eat something that wasn't Burger King chicken nuggets, I knew that I would soon miss the city once again. I spent most the flight home in a Dramamine-induced coma, but Rebekah and I reminisced about our trip during the short periods I was awake. We also started talking about the other journeys we wanted to take and what order we would accomplish them. Naturally Paris came first, followed by Hong Kong and, eventually, Shanghai as well.

Suddenly, growing older didn't seem so bad now that I had someone to grow older with. If I was in season five of *Friends*, I still had a lot to look forward to. New homes, new experiences, new members of the family; they were all ahead of us. The difference, of course, being that there were no writers behind the scenes creating a timeline for our lives.

When I proposed to Rebekah, I presented her with a hollow book that housed her engagement ring. While I knew that I was cheesy, I said we'd fill that book with the adventures we'd share and I meant it. As the wheels of our double-decker plane touched back down in Los Angeles, another chapter of our story concluded. One chapter down but so many left to go.

35
Tokyo DisneyLand of Snacks

It doesn't take long when walking around the streets of Tokyo to realize some fundamental differences in culture when compared to America. One of the first things Rebekah and I noticed while visiting the city on our honeymoon was how clean the sidewalks and roads were. Even in the most populated and trafficked areas, you'd be hard pressed to find any errant debris.

This stood in stark contrast to what we're used to in America. Sure, most of us are more courteous and don't make a habit of littering, yet it takes a huge team and, famously, a trash can every 20 feet to keep the Disney Parks clean. What accounts for this huge difference?

After studying this phenomenon a little closer, we discovered part of the answer. On the whole, Japanese citizens don't make a habit of eating on the go. It wasn't until my wife spent several blocks looking for a trash can to dispose of her banana peel that we picked up on this fact, but it actually explained a lot. Every time we'd go into a fast food restaurant on our trip (which was a lot, since I'm the worst), a majority of the seating would be occupied by patrons who had already finished their meals but were spending time reading a newspaper or talking to a friend. Coming from a place obsessed with consistently upgrading products to increase portability, this was as refreshing as it was odd.

Whatever it was that prevented people from eating on the go in the rest of Tokyo apparently goes out in the window once the berm of the Tokyo Disneyland Resort is breached. Where as seeing a person in Shinjuku carrying so much as a cup of coffee with them was a rare sight, making it 50 paces without seeing someone reaching into their popcorn bucket (with lanyard attached) was equally as remarkable. As it turns out, Tokyo Disney could easily be dubbed "The Land of Snacks."

If you were writing an essay proving this theory (which I suppose I am), the first case in point would be TDL's renowned popcorn selections. In the stateside parks, popcorn is pretty much kept to the classic version, but maybe a kettle or caramel variant makes its way in every once in a while. Meanwhile, Tokyo has so many flavors they actually rotate out seasonal flavors to grant even more variety.

Having worked at a movie theatre for over 11 years of my life, I don't much fancy popcorn any longer. Yet, on my latest journey, my wife and I tried six different types, which doesn't even represent all of them. Considering that they cost over $3 each, we skipped over the more common flavors like caramel and even some others like strawberry or curry. But, after devouring the entire box in little to no time, we kept notes and an ongoing ranking. Here were the results:

6) Soy Sauce and Butter- This seemed like it should have been a home run given the combination of umami flavors. The problem is that it doesn't much taste like either. While still being wildly delicious, it would be immensely better if real butter and soy sauce were applied on top.

5) Sea Salt and Black Pepper- The only reason this ranks so low is because it's not as original as some of the others. It is still definitely worth eating.

4) Honey- This one gets points just for theming as it is only served outside of Pooh's Hunny Hunt. It seems like it would be a more creative choice, but it is remarkably similar to the caramel corn we all know and love. However, to be perfectly honest, it was a toss up between this and the third place flavor.

3) Soda- During our visit in April of 2014, this was the seasonal flavor being offered. When you purchase soda-flavored popcorn, you may expect it to be brown like cola or clear like cream soda. Instead, the kernels were coated in green. This was easily the most confusing flavor of popcorn we tried and might be the most confusing flavor of anything I've ever had. Whenever we thought we'd nailed down what it tasted like, it changed. Every bite was delicious, but strange. Some of the comparisons we threw around were bubblegum, Sprite, and Fruit Loops... but never at the same time.

2) Milk Tea- This actually may have been my winner, but it was a close race and my wife voted the other way. The milk tea flavor is exclusive to the Cape Cod area of American Waterfront where Duffy, Shellie May, and whatever other characters they've invented since then reside. With almost no hint of actual tea, the popcorn taste much more like berries, which makes a lot of sense considering the milk tea sold near by is a mixed berry flavor.

1) Corn Potage- I honestly don't recall if this was seasonal or not, but we also got it in Tokyo DisneySea. The very idea of corn-flavored popcorn is admittedly ridiculous and bizarre, yet here it sits at the top of our list. Apparently corn pottage is a type of soup prevalent in Japan. Before we Google'd that fact upon getting back to our hotel, we assumed the popcorn was just made to taste like creamed corn. — close enough. Still, with a golden coating and scrumptiously sweet flavor, the corn-flavored popcorn surprised us and made us very glad we didn't pass it over like we nearly did.

***

So over the course of four days, we consumed six boxes of popcorn. While I'm not exactly proud of that, I do have some excuses. First, they were delicious. Second, there were two of us splitting each box. And thirdly, between the small portions served for meals (or "sets" as combos are known in Japan) and the numerous other snack-worthy items in the parks, we treated the resort's dining more like we The International Food and Wine Festival at Epcot.

To be fair, there were a number of decently sized and decently priced meal options we had during our visit, ranging from hot dogs to chicken curry. However, what we quickly discovered is that it was way more fun and not much more expensive to just eat random smaller items throughout the day than attempt to adhere to a typical three-meal structure. We stuck to that plan for the second half of our Tokyo Disneyland trip and appropriately dubbed these days "Snack Days," because we're *clearly* insanely clever.

As we'd walk around the parks, we literally checked every menu of every restaurant, counter, and cart along the way. If something sounded good, we'd either pick it up then and there or make a mental note to return when hunger stuck. I also tried to make a point of eating my snacks in short enough succession to allow my bottle of Coke to last me through all of them.

Of the numerous culinary treats I got to enjoy over those two days, my absolute favorite was the pork rice roll found in Tokyo DisneySea. A common practice throughout the resort and all of Tokyo is to display plastic versions of the food served in a case. This is presumably so that picky foreigners like me can see what they're getting themselves into before ordering. The plastic version of the roll made it look like an almost pretzel-type bun that was then stuffed with the titular pork and rice. Instead, I discovered that it was actually sticky rice wrapped in teriyaki-glazed bacon. Need I say more?

Pretty much everyone I tell about this snack says the same thing: "I thought they ate healthy over there?" I guess not in Disneyland, they don't. After a single bite, the pork rice roll became my new favorite thing ever. I even made my wife get another so I could have back the bite I mistakenly offered to her.

Every once in a while, photos will make their way around social media of some of the fantastic things Tokyo Disneyland offers that we are severally lacking in the states. One such photo is of the Little Green Men dumplings served near the Japanese version of Toy Story Midway Mania.

These dumplings are similar to mochi, as the exterior is rice-based but the filling was more of a pudding than the ice cream-esque mochi found in America. Served in threes, each dumpling resembles the famous aliens and each order contains one custard, one chocolate, and one strawberry version. While I liked the idea more than the actual product, my wife was far more enthusiastic.

Some of our other selections were a little less creative but no less scrumptious. Pork gyoza (potstickers), both teriyaki and spicy chicken legs, and churros covered in orange flavored sugar were all eaten and given positive reviews. My only disappointment was that, during my first visit, there had been a sesame churro available that I had excited my wife about. Unfortunately, the churro was no more, but she did have a chocolate churro with strawberry sugar in its place — that seemed to take some of the pain away.

During the rest of our trip to Tokyo, my wife resented my lack of culinary adventure. Since I could at least read the English names of the food items and was still in the safety of Disney, I figured the least I could do was venture a bit out of my comfort zone a little bit at a time — trying curry was a major accomplishment for me. As it turns out, I was handsomely rewarded for my efforts considering that everything I consumed was amazing. It almost made me want to try all sorts of other dishes when we went back into the heart of Tokyo... I said "almost." Still, it goes to show me that my wife was right all along. But I guess every man learns that fact while on his honeymoon, huh?

36
Ghibli

Of all the sights I got to experience on my first visit to Tokyo, The Studio Ghibli museum was regrettably not one of them. At that time, I didn't realize the popularity of the attraction nor the strict ticketing procedures that went along with it. The closest I got to figuring out how to obtain entry was to purchase a ticket from an automated machine located in various Tokyo convenience stores. However, when I tracked down a location near my hotel, I walked in only to discover that the machine was entirely in Japanese with no translation option.

For those who don't know, Studio Ghibli is a Japanese animation house founded in part by Hayao Miyazaki. If that name sounds familiar, it is because he is known as one of the all-time masters of animation and one whose name can appropriately be spoken in the same breath as Walt Disney's. That's why it only made sense when Disney entered into a deal to distribute the studio's films in America. One of Ghibli's most popular characters, Totoro, even made a cameo in *Toy Story 3* (he belonged to

Bonnie and looks like a cross between a cat and Grimace).

I've never been a big fan of anime or "Japan-imation," but there was something uniquely different about the Ghibli films I saw. The more I explored from the studio, the more I kicked myself for not looking into visiting the museum when I had the chance. Luckily, when the opportunity came around the second time, I remedied my mistake.

One of the first things Rebekah and I did while planning our honeymoon was research how to get tickets for the Ghibli Museum prior to embarking on our trip. After looking through several less-than-helpful websites, my Canadian friend, Cara-Lynn, sent me info on a travel agency in Torrance that sold admissions. According to them, the museum offers a certain number of tickets to various countries and then those tickets are divided amongst a select few sources. This meant that, as soon as tickets for certain dates became available, they would quickly be snatched up.

Since we were going to be in Tokyo for 12 days, we figured we had plenty of dates to choose from. However, we were barely lucky enough to find one day where tickets were available, even so far in advance. Making the situation even odder was that the tickets were merely printed on plain paper, but the agency insisted that the museum was strict about copies. Thus, they would mail you these originals for $11 or we could drive the 45 minutes to Torrance to pick them up. We opted for the latter.

Incidentally, for all this rigmarole, the tickets themselves were only $15 dollars each. Another interesting stipulation was that our passports would need to be shown and would have to match the corresponding ticket. I guess it's good we didn't go through the Canadian site we found that seemed far more straightforward than ours in the states…

We visited the museum near the end of our trip and after our four days of adventure in Tokyo Disneyland. As much as we enjoyed our treks out into random parts of Tokyo, it was nice to have an actual goal in mind for the day, especially when there was some Disney connection. That morning, we woke up relatively earlier and headed out to the train station, our first stop on the journey to Ghibli.

Soon after exiting the train, we discovered that the Ghibli Museum sits in a very interesting area. From the train station, signs featuring Totoro lead you down a small street about one kilometer to the museum itself. Surrounded by large, lush trees, the building sits slightly recessed from the road. So much so, that you might pass it if not for the sign just off the sidewalk.

As you draw closer, you see a giant version of Totoro standing behind glass. This also marks one of the few photo spots of the experience since photography is only permitted in the exterior portions of the attraction. Several employees stand at the entry gates to greet ticketholders and turn away the presumable hundreds who assumed there would be some walk-up availability.

Once inside, we were given actual 35mm filmstrips that were framed in cardboard (about the size of a bookmark) along with a map of the exhibits. A short hall then led us to the main lobby where the many levels of the building were exposed. Straight ahead was The Saturn Theatre where each guest got to enjoy one screening of a short animated film. To our right was a hands-on exhibit explaining the principles of animation and some special effects.

While we walked through the exhibit, we were treated to and intrigued by several delightful displays. These ranged from many of the simple machines that can be found in the Animation Building at Disney California Adventure to more advanced demonstrations that were like a science fair for cartoons. We were even able to project the images from filmstrips onto a screen and see them in action.

Upstairs was an exhibit that occupies the majority of the floor. Once walking through the entrance, it was as though you had walked into the working offices of Studio Ghibli animators. The entire area was littered with hand drawn images from Ghibli works as well as working animator tools you could try for yourself. If you wanted to, you could potentially spend hours just searching through all of the materials on display. Instead, we followed the slow but steadily moving line through the faux-offices and made our way to the rest of the museum.

Even with all of the strict capacity limitations, the museums popular areas do tend to get crowded. For example, there is typically a queue formed just to enter the gift shop (a la The Wizarding World of Harry Potter). Yet some areas, like the lovely rooftop garden area that houses a statue of the Robot Soldier from *Castle in the Sky*, allow you the space to relax and breathe. Still some parts of the museum, namely The Straw Hat Café, proved too in demand for us to visit.

We reentered the building through the Catbus room, which featured a giant plushy version of the Catbus from *My Neighbor Totoro* that children 12 and under could play on. From there, we headed down to the ground floor only to climb back up, though this time using the intentionally cramped spiral staircase that makes you feel as though you were climbing out of a birdcage. After another quick lap around, we headed back down to the Saturn Theatre to see our film.

When the lady at the front desk told us that our filmstrips would be our ticket to the film (since they only allowed one screening per guest per day) we thought this meant that we might have to give up our fancy bookmarks in exchange for admission. I wasn't so sure I wanted to part with mine, but after observing how others proceeded in, we realized that the employee would merely stamp the cardboard area to denote our entrance. After watching the film, I was surely glad we had made it in.

The film screening on the day of our visit was *The Whale Hunt*, written and directed by Hayao Miyazaki himself. I learned later that the film was created exclusively for the museum, as are all of the shorts that screen in The Saturn Theatre. Over the course of the film's 16 minute runtime, we see children go from building a ship made from the toy blocks in their classroom to encountering a giant (but friendly) whale. As the credits rolled, I thought about how easily the same story could have been made as a Disney Animation or Pixar short, given the amount of heart and humor it contained.

After a bit more exploring, Rebekah and I headed out of the museum and back to the train station. Along the way, we talked about our favorite parts and watched as people followed the Totoro signs towards the museum. Part of me wanted to stop and ensure them that they were in for a treat.

The thing about the Ghibli Museum is how it's just the right amount of whimsy for me. In my opinion, sometimes things that are supposed to be fun can ultimately be annoying. For me, Zonkos in the Hogsmeade section of Universal's Islands of Adventure falls into the latter category. Though cleverly detailed, the obnoxious tricks that pop out, make noise, or otherwise annoy during your walk through deter me from visiting again.

While some part of me feared that The Ghibli Museum might hold some of these same characteristics, I quickly learned that this was not the case. Though the layout is admittedly confusing, never is there a dead end just for the sake of fooling you. Even the birdcage staircase actually has payoff as you reach the top.

Instead, I'd compare the museum to the Disney parks. The amount of education that can be garnered from a tour of the exhibits that call to mind attractions in Disney's Hollywood Studios, Disney California Adventure, and even Epcot. Additionally, the level of not only detail but also interactivity is on par with a Disney offering. There almost isn't anything you can't do… except take pictures. Overall, my visit to The Ghibli Museum only furthered my appreciation for Miyazaki, his films, and the art of animation.

37
Billy Hill

The great irony of Disneyland is that fans think of certain attractions as being holy while still clamoring for new ones to be built. When attractions like The Country Bear Jamboree in Disneyland or Mr. Toad's Wild Ride in Magic Kingdom do close, there's the inevitable outcry at first, but eventually the fervor dies down. Though these closures can be sad, at the end of the day, they're just animatronics losing their jobs and not actually people. That's what makes the case of Billy Hill and the Hillbillies a bit different.

I remember seeing Billy Hill for the first time back when The Golden Horseshoe still served cheeseburgers. I'm not sure if my father knew a show was going to start up or just happened to like the look of the venue, but we took our seats and the Hillbillies came out while we were only a few bites into our food. The Billies' show combined country western (the real stuff, not Florida Georgia Line or Taylor Swift) with a surprisingly unique brand of comedy. Heck, even the name of the show was partially a joke, as all four members on stage were named Billy Hill and had the nametags to prove it. Even at that age, I found their show entertaining and their shtick caused younger me to giggle with enjoyment... even if I got far more of their jokes as I grew older. Yet, as much as I liked the Hillbillies, once I became an Annual Passholder I learned that some people were far more into the show than I was.

One of the original hosts of *The Disneyland Gazette* podcast, Chuck, was a huge fan of the Hillbillies. He even had a custom-made shirt featuring the lead Billy/Elvis impersonator, Kirk Wall, with his fiddle bow up his nostril and the tagline, "You won't see this in the brochure," printed below. That joke was actually a reference to the show where Billy would stop the performance once this nasal accident occurred and talk about how such an image would never make a good promotion for the park, but it also pretty much sums up The Billies' experience at Disneyland.

Before my time, Billy Hill and the Hillbillies had a number of venues, as they would often acknowledge in their new home of The Golden Horseshoe. Over the years, the show had also moved timeslots a lot and been shortened to accommodate more performances. When the Horseshoe was down for refurbishment, the show would pop up elsewhere. One time, that meant The Hillbilies materializing just outside of the Hungry Bear restaurant. On the first day of the refurb schedule, I went with Chuck and his wife, Leigh, to catch the Critter Country edition of their show. Since the times guide was fairly vague about the location of the show, several of the Hillbillies fans stood around asking each other if anyone knew anything more than the rest of us.

Eventually the gentleman appeared and, in true Billy fashion, congratulated us on finding them. Their set that day consisted of some more pop covers than their typical sets in the Horseshoe, including "These Boots Are Made For Walkin' " by Nancy Sinatra. It was a fun set, but you could tell the boys were excited to return to their home stage.

Not too long after, The Hillbillies were displaced once again; this time permanently. In a decision aimed at making use of the area that once housed The Festival of Fools, the Billies took the stage in Big Thunder Ranch starting in 2012. Part of their set includes a bit where the group's resident fiddle player recreates the sound of the a train going past the platform, creatively referred to as "The Train Thing." While in The Golden

Horseshoe, their might be a moment where a riverboat's horn could be heard from The Rivers of America just outside, leading Kirk — I mean... Billy — to remark, "That's not the train, that's the Twain." Unfortunately, their new venue sat right next to the tracks of the Disneyland Railroad. When a train would inevitably come through and disrupt the boys' show, they'd make the best of it by trying to get the entire audience to wave at them in an effort to freak out the passengers onboard.

In the winter of 2013, Disney debuted what was called "The Jingle Jangle Jamboree." That show featured Billy Hill and the (Holiday) Hillbillies performing a set of some unique Christmastime selections amongst a sea of standards. The finale even included a medley of carols and a cameo by The Country Bears. During that incarnation of the show's run, a post on the Disney Parks Blog announced that Billy Hill and the Hillbillies would be retiring come January.

The word "retiring" in the original post caught many fans' attention. Much like the company-wide e-mails that go out wishing an ousted co-worker, "The best of luck in their future endeavors," I think it's fair to say that the general consensus was that the Hillbillies departure was not their idea. This notion was given more legitimacy when a group going by the name of Krazy Kirk and The Hillbillies was announced for a New Year's Eve show at nearby Knott's Berry Farm. During that performance, Wall made several jokes about the situation, but made it clear that they loved Disneyland and appreciated their time there.

To be fair, it is possible that The Billies were fed up with their treatment and decided to leave, but I don't think we'll ever know what happened behind closed doors in Anaheim. Billy Hill and the Hillbillies performed their last show on January 6th, 2014. For their final set, Big Thunder Ranch was packed with hundreds of adoring fans there for one last show. Though they were dressed in Christmas colors and announced over the PA as the Holiday Hillbillies, the boys performed some of their best-known tunes. When it came time for the Country Bears to come out, which normally signaled the end of the song, the fans let their disappointment known. This lead Kirk to joke that he had somehow made Disneyland fans hate The Country Bears.

The medley of holiday songs didn't end the set that night. Instead, The Billies played one more song. Speaking to the crowd, Krazy Kirk, as he would soon be known, echoed many of the same sentiments he offered during the Knott's show, saying that, if it weren't for Disneyland, he wouldn't have met his band mates or even his wife. To close out the show, The Hillbillies performed a song they hoped Disney wouldn't mind them covering since it was a one of theirs: "You've Got a Friend In Me" from *Toy Story*.

A short time later, Krazy Kirk and The Hillbillies announced a semi-regular schedule at Knott's Berry Farm. Though at each step of the way, the band members were quick to note that their stint at Knott's wasn't a done deal, the group still performs there today. Having only been to Knott's Berry Farm once, I've never gotten to go revisit the boys in person. I'd be remiss at point if I didn't note that the group performing at Knott's is just one group of the several performers that played a role in the band over the years. This unfortunately meant that some of those other Billies never got to experience the same fanfare and warm farewell that the Knott's-bound crew received.

Several Disney fans turn to the parks for nostalgia, which it offers in spades. When children and adults alike visit, they expect to see their favorite shows and attractions there waiting for them. Unfortunately, that's not always the case and Billy Hill and the Hillbillies are just one example of the never-completed park's nature to evolve. Though it's often quoted to the point of cliché, in times like these fans are best to take the advice of the legendary Dr. Seuss: "Don't cry because it's over; smile because it happened"... But you won't find that in the brochure.

38
Magic Castle

In the heart of Hollywood, just a couple of blocks from the Disney-owned movie palace The El Capitan, sits a historic structure that contains as much lure and intrigue as Disneyland's famed Club 33. On a small street that features a handful of apartments and in the shadow of the shopping center that houses the Oscars sits an unassuming castle a few yards up a hill. At first glace, you might assume the building was just home to some rich Los Angeles eccentric, but The Magic Castle is actually a restaurant, lounge, and stage for some of the world's best illusionists.

I had actually heard of the Magic Castle when my mother dated someone whose ex used to perform there. Back in those days, the venue was exclusively for magicians and their guests. However, in recent years and under the management of Neil Patrick Harris (yes, that Neil Patrick Harris, in case there was any doubt), the club has loosened its policies and now anyone with money can enter. Even with these changes, the Castle remains one of the most sought after invitations in town.

The Magic Castle had eluded me for years. For a time, the building was actually the view from my apartment, sitting less than a block away from my front door. Yet my journey to the Castle began with a series of near misses.

First I was promised a visit in exchange for getting a member of the Castle into Club 33. Unfortunately, due to busy schedules, she never had a chance to fulfill her end of the deal before her membership had lapsed. Next, my good friend and former roommate, Stephanie, informed me that her boyfriend had gotten a job there and would be able to get us in whenever we want. You can probably guess how this ended, right? Yup — they broke up. Around that same time, I had another offer to go... except that the person offering was notoriously flaky and so it was no surprise that that never came to fruition either.

Not long after that, I moved out of Hollywood and away from The Magic Castle. Since I didn't see it everyday, the thought of visiting had mostly vanished from my mind. However, sometimes I would see photos of people who had visited (taken outside since photography is forbidden inside... for the most part) posted on Facebook and feel a sense of envy come over me. Then, finally, my chance to explore the Castle arrived.

One day, my friend Josh called and asked if Rebekah and I would be interested in going to The Magic Castle with some friends of his. It turns out that one of them — who is also a Disney fan — was a magician and was thusly entitled to bring guests into the club. I accepted his invitation before it had fully left his lips and quickly told my wife the excited news. She proceeded to ask me, "What's that?"

Despite my poor attempt to explain the place to her (having never been), the initials 'NPH' were enough to excite her about the evening. The first thing we did was look up the club's dress code to ensure we had the correct attire for our visit. When that night rolled around, I donned my suit — the same one I wore to both my wedding and *Glee* prom —and my wife wore one of her favorite dresses and a pair of heels for our brief brush with the well to do.

There were several things I was nervous about as we drove down to Hollywood. First was the fact that my filthy Toyota Yaris with body damage would surely look out of place rolling up to the mandatory valet that manned the Castle's parking lot. Similarly, I feared that my H&M suit would look silly amongst a room of Armani. Finally, I was concerned that I might be dragged into the show of one of the acts and forced to participate all while displaying a smile on my face. The first two proved relatively unfounded, but that third one...

As we got closer to our reservation time, Bekah and I were within 5 miles of our destination. Then traffic suddenly came to a halt as I had fallen victim to one of the most rookie Los Angeles mistakes: I had forgotten to check the Hollywood Bowl schedule. Inching along, I tried to convince myself that it was still too early in the season for the venue to be open, but soon t-shirt vendors walking through the slow moving traffic proved me wrong.

Like it does, traffic immediately cleared as soon as we passed the Bowl's parking lot and we were able to reach the Magic Castle's entrance five minutes later. By this time, we were a good half hour late. That's when a new problem presented itself.

Before we could enter, we were stopped and informed that the club was currently at capacity unless we were with a magician performing that night. Instead, the employee gave us tickets and told us to return closer to 10 P.M. as people started to leave. I called Josh to tell him what had happened and his magician friend tried his best to get us in to no avail. This only served to make me more uncomfortable, as it seemed like I was trying to flaunt my importance to the bouncer when I clearly had none. To combat this, I peppered the conversation with phrases like, "No, it's ok," "My fault," and, "Yeah I'll just see you guys later."

After a few hours of killing time at the Hollywood and Highland Center and showing Rebekah where I used to live, we made our way back up the hill to the Castle. By that time, a short line had formed in front of the club and we took our place at the end. However, since our tickets had been issued first we got to go in a few minutes later.

When you first enter the Castle, it feels like you've stepped into a library you'd find in *Beauty and the Beast* or *Clue*. It's a rather small room with no clear path as to where you'd head after paying your cover charge. But once you're given the magic words and repeat them to a statue that resides on one of the shelves, the bookcase opens allowing you to proceed into the lounge. *Now* it feels like you're in a magic castle.

In terms of atmosphere, the Magic Castle is a strange mix of posh and playful. For example, although the patrons are dressed in sports coats, the bathrooms make fake fart noises. The labyrinth of a building contains three main showrooms of varying sizes but it seems that nearly any corner you find yourself in has a trick being performed or some other attraction to entertain you.

I was finally able to meet up with Josh and his party near one of the showrooms. It was there that I also spotted Stephanie's ex, Brandon. After a little catching up — including introducing him to my wife — he offered to get me seats in the show that was just beginning. A few moments later, Rebekah and I got to experience our first magic show in the Castle.

Mere minutes into the show came that part of the performance where the magicians (plural in this case) come into the audience to find volunteers. Despite my sitting next to a beautiful woman who would make fabulous assistant (if I do say so myself), I was selected to come on stage. Ugh. My duty was to tie one gentleman to a chair using thick rope. Of course, the directions given to me asked me to make it as tight as possible, which my scrawny arms did their best to comply with.

Despite that highly awkward moment, the show was enjoyable overall. Brandon greeted us at the exit and again offered us seats in the theatre next door. This was a smaller auditorium and so we were seated right up front. As you'd probably expect, this led to me being dragged up to help out once again. Luckily for me, this time it was just a card trick and I even got to keep the signed card he made appear. However, my favorite part of the performance was a segment in which the magician utilized the score from *Monsters Inc.* as his soundtrack. Incidentally, this was only one of numerous Disney tie-ins we found throughout the Castle.

Near the exit to that second showroom, there was a window dedicated to Robert and Richard Sherman, similar in style to the ones found on Main Street USA. Not far away from that was an automated marionette display like those found in a penny arcade. When the button was pressed, the puppets behind the glass dance to a song titled "The Magic Castle Shuffle" written by none other than Richard Sherman — clearly the Disney Legend had an affinity for the club.

Somewhat hidden in the lower part of the Castle is an interesting piece of Disney Parks' history. Down in a small hallway sits what is described as the original diorama Imagineer Yale Gracey built to demonstrate the Pepper's Ghost effect to Walt. That visual trick is most famously utilized in the Disney classic, The Haunted Mansion. In fact, a sign for the attraction hangs on the wall and a short video explains the illusion before showing the diorama in action.

To end our evening, our entire party headed into a relatively dead portion of the Castle where music was emanating from. In that room, much like in The Haunted Mansion, sat a piano seemingly playing itself. However, tickling the ivories was actually the Castle's house spirit, Irma. The great thing about Irma is that she actually takes requests. Being the Disney geeks that we are, we asked her to treat us to everything from "There's a Great Big Beautiful Tomorrow" to "Baroque Hoedown." She even knew the theme to *Fraggle Rock* and performed a haunting version of Rihanna's "Stay" (she apparently didn't know "We Found Love" — a rare miss for the poltergeist piano prodigy). For having passed away decades earlier, Irma sure had kept up with the contemporary hits.

Before leaving, we snapped photos outside of all of us in our classy outfits and sporting huge smiles. After getting my car back and adjusting the seat to its far-forward position (I'm short), Rebekah and I headed home, making sure to avoid passing the Bowl this time around. On our short trek back, we talked about our overall impressions, most of which included our surprise to find so much Disney within the castle walls.

In retrospect, it actually makes a lot of sense that the Magic Castle and the Disney Parks share some history. The most obvious connection is the castle element, though this one doesn't belong to any princess. But, more than that, is the fact that Walt, his Imagineers, and the performers at the Castle all create magic before our very eyes. Whether on a small theatre stage, on screen, or at the theme parks, it's not only illusions and trickery on display but creativity and wit. It's no wonder that Mr. Harris is such a fan of both.

Like Club 33, The Magic Castle isn't a place most Disney fans will ever get to go to. That makes me a little sad, knowing how much they'd enjoy it if they could. But, for those lucky enough to explore the chambers, I challenge you to experience the whimsy the Castle offers without thinking of Walt and his Imagineers.

39
24 Hours

Sitting in the lobby of the Grand Californian, it is emptier than I have ever seen it. So much so, that it almost seems smaller than normal and I can't quite get my bearings as to where everything is. Maybe this is because, while I have walked through the hotel probably a hundred times in the past, I have never actually driven directly to it. Then again, I have also never been here at 5 A.M., but today Disney is hosting their "Rock Your Disney Side" event in which the park will remain open for a full 24 hours.

This is the to be the third such stunt performed by the resort in recent times; once for Leap Day in 2012 and again Memorial Day weekend 2013 to celebrate a "Monstrous Summer" kick-off. While the idea of being in Disney at such odd hours seemed novel, my fear of the large crowds and grad night-esque atmosphere was enough to stop me from attending either event. I might have skipped this one as well except that I was asked to cover it as media for LaughingPlace.com.

I have been working for the Laughing Place for a few months now, writing articles about various Disney-related functions and news. Usually this just involves me sitting inconspicuously, using my phone as a voice recorder, and jotting down the timestamp whenever a good quote comes up that I can use for my piece. Then I go home, listen back to my audio, find an angle, write the article, and send it off to Benji who plays the role of editor.

Benji and I have been friends since meeting at the 2009 D23 Expo. He even let me stay with him while I visited Walt Disney World back when he lived in Orlando. When the site was getting ready to expand, he asked if I knew of anyone who would be interested in helping out. After offering a couple of names, I humbly submitted myself for the position.

Even though I am a bit anxious about this latest media event, I've sucked up any trepidation I had in an effort not to let my friend down. Though, when I first accepted the assignment, my role was going to be taking photos and running the @laughing_place Twitter for the first part of the day. Meanwhile another reporter, Doug, would be doing the "heavy lifting"… whatever that might be.

Yesterday, Doug called me to go over our media itinerary. As it turns out, he is going to have to take off before noon, leaving me to do the majority of the events Disney has lined up for us. Doug walked me through the itinerary, which will include interviews with Imagineers, ambassadors, and artists. Suddenly it seems that I will be upgraded from iPhone intern to legitimate press.

***

Knowing that I was in for an interesting day, I jotted down everything you just read onto a legal notepad I kept in my bag for just such an occasion of inspiration. Moments after I put my pad away, Doug walked in the front entrance of the Grand and greeted our media host, Christopher. From there, the three of us headed through Downtown Disney and into the esplanade where tired guests were waiting for the parks to open at 6 A.M..

When I first met Christopher, he said that he had heard me on the podcast. This would be flattering except that I'm not on the *Laughing Place Podcast* and so I assumed he was just lying. But, no harm, no foul, I suppose. Later, he corrected himself and noted that he had actually heard me on *The Disney Gazette* podcast and, suddenly, what seemed like an empty compliment was actually extremely exciting. I then asked him why the Gazette never got invited to such events, for which he had no answer. Oh well.

Chris escorted us past security and into the media area that had been set up in between the two parks. There, I received my official media credentials, a disc that would be used to record my interviews, and even a quick layer of make-up (at Doug's insistence), so that I would look better on camera. Who knew Disney fan-sites got such Hollywood treatment?

Doug was handling the first interview — a cooking demo on Main Street USA — that was taking place just before park opening. While he headed to that appointment with our media host, I remained in my press pen in order to get video of the kick-off moment. As the crowd got ready to countdown until the turnstiles would open, Josh Gad (most notably Olaf from *Frozen*, but "the guy from that short-lived NBC show about the President" to me) took the stage, as fireworks were set off in the distance.

After snapping a few photos of Gad and some of the other sites to see in the esplanade, I headed into Disneyland proper to meet up with Doug again before he left. Just as I was about to head to where his interview was, he called and asked me to instead meet in The Opera House. However, when I got there, I noticed the attraction was closed and a Cast Member stood out front of it. Being used to what this means for normal guests, I stopped and was about to take out my phone to call Doug before Christopher saw me and ushered me in. It turns out the reason the room was closed was because it was set up as a lounge for media with free food and beverages.

Since I'm not big on breakfast, I merely poked around a pasty while attempting to e-mail Doug the video I had taken of the opening ceremony. After we finished eating, he turned the itinerary over to me and headed out for the day. My first interview wasn't for several hours and so I told Christopher I'd just meet up with him later.

After several laps around Disneyland and Disney California Adventure, taking photos and tweeting out cosplay, wait times, and other various happenings, it was nearly time to meet back up with Christopher. My first interview was with Megan Navarette, one of the Disneyland Ambassadors. The night prior, when Doug had gone over who I would interviewing, this one wasn't mentioned, leaving me no time to research or think of questions. Further complicating things was the fact that our itinerary didn't give much info on what we would be talking to Megan about.

It turned out that the topic was "Summer Time and Classic Attractions." If you're like me, you see no real correlation between these two things. As I got mic'd up and ready to go on camera, I broke down and asked Megan just what the heck I was supposed to be asking her about. The answer was really a great piece of Disney spin: That year, Disneyland hadn't opened any new attractions and so they were highlighting the summer season as a great time to revisit the older ones. Alright then.

After putting it off for as long as I could, I just had to dive into the awkwardness that was looking into the camera, introducing myself, and introducing my guest. That all went well enough, but in the middle of my first question I froze and had to start over. Luckily for me, being a Disney Ambassador meant that Megan knew how to take whatever incoherent and awful question I had just asked and find a way to answer while inserting the messages Disney wanted her to convey. Surprisingly, my comment about people having to wait four hours in the heat to meet Anna and Elsa even made it past the Disney censors in the edit bay.

Once my mic was removed and disc returned, I walked back over to Christopher shaking my head. He apparently didn't hear the interview. I vented to him about how awful it was as we headed over to my next appointment, interviewing an Imagineer while riding Big Thunder Mountain Railroad.

To recap the pros and cons of this particular set, the first pro is that I could think of enough questions to ask an Imagineer about the ride. However, the biggest con is that I had to ask these questions while riding a freaking roller coaster. Disney had closed off one half of the attraction for this media op and had equipped a train with a GoPro camera on the front, a mounted camera in the middle, and lights on one of the cars near the back where the interview would be conducted.

There was a rotating cast of Imagineers participating and I ended up sitting with Ray Spencer, who had worked on the then-recent refurbishment of the ride. Before the ride took off, I was able to ask a couple of the questions I had thought of: What lead them to do such a major refurbishment? How do you balance keeping what makes the attraction such a classic while creating a new experience? Were there really plans to change the theme to The Lone Ranger had the film not totally tanked?

I attempted to ask a couple more questions during our ride, but the loud panels along the lift hills made that all but impossible. Instead, most of the video is just me playing up my enjoyment of the ride for whatever audience might see the video. Still, Ray took the time to point our some of the new effects and I pointed out what my favorite part of the ride is. Spoiler: It's the long right turn that seems that it may never end… kind of like my interview with Megan.

With two interviews down, it was time for my final one of the day. Incidentally, it was also the one I prepared the most for… or so I thought. I had known of the artist, Noah, from my days as a Vinylmation collector. At that time, it also seemed like any piece of artwork on display in Off the Page that wasn't Thomas Kinkade's was his.

I started my first question by noting that, to me, Noah's artwork made him a perfect fit for the "Rock Your Disney Side" campaign. Much like himself (covered in tattoos, for one), Noah's art often stepped outside the norms of what Disney pieces tend to look like. Because of this, I found that many people who might not otherwise hang a painting of Mickey Mouse on their walls *would* given Noah's spin on the classic character.

Eventually, we segued to the giant chalk drawing that he had done for the event that was sitting on the ground next to us. This is when he mentioned it was part of a spin-off campaign called "Rock Your Disney Sidewalk" that encouraged kids to use creativity to make art in their neighborhoods. It turns out that's really what the interview was supposed to be about, so I guess it's good I eventually worked it in.

Luckily, Noah didn't seem to mind that I ventured off the beaten path a bit. Especially since this was also his last interview for the day, he seemed to appreciate having different questions to answer. Incidentally, I ended up sitting next to him and his family on a flight back from Orlando a few months later and he claimed to remember the interview.

With that, I had completed my first ever round of media interviews. Huzzah! I gave my disc to Chris, who would then take care of all the paperwork Disney needed in order to send us the videos we shot. After spending another few hours in the parks tweeting for the Laughing Place and The Disneyland Gazette, I was relieved when other members from each site arrived to take over. Before heading out, I was able to meet up with my friend Chris (not the media host — different Chris) and the two of us watched one of the Frozen Sing-a-Long screenings that were being held in the then-Muppet*Vision theatre.

After the movie, I was exhausted. With the long and sure-to-be-horrendous drive back to Los Angeles ahead of me, I walked back to the Grand Californian to retrieve my car. Once inside, I took off my bag and media lanyard, threw them on the passenger seat, and headed back towards the 5.

You may think it's strange to call this chapter "24 Hours" if I spent just over half of that in the park that day. In addition to the fact that it felt like double that, the whole experience was 24 hours for me. From the time Doug called to break the news to me and got my nerves working overtime to the time I headed home for well-deserved nap, it had been a very full day. While it's painfully hard for me to watch the videos from that day, I can still say I was proud of myself. Not only had I rocked my Disney side, I had rocked my brave side.

40
The Office Age and After

If there's a theme to my employment history, it's that I start with something I love at the center, choose a job somewhere in its radius, and then attempt to work my way inward. I guess that's a positive way to spin my storied movie theatre managing career that somehow segued into being an extra which then turned into... whatever I'm doing now. In all cases, I wanted a gig that was not only under the umbrella of "entertainment" but would also entertain me along the way.

With that logic, the question of why I don't work for Disney inevitably comes up again. However, the truth is that I feel like I kind of did for a while. Over the past year I surely spent more time in Disneyland than nearly 90% of non-Cast Members. In fact, I made Disneyland my office for a few months.

Following my bang-up reporting of the Rock Your Disney Side 24-hour event for Laughing Place, Benji started sending me out on some more assignments. Some of these were in Burbank (like when I covered the press junket for *Big Hero 6)*, others were in Hollywood (like when I got to interview Fall Out Boy at El Capitan), but the majority of press events I attended were still down in Anaheim.

Even on days I wasn't "working" an event at the resort, I found it fitting to write this book while "on location," as it were. It's certainly weird for me to consider Disneyland less distracting than my bedroom, but it was. For one, there was no internet in the parks (unless I went to one of the hotels or the Starbucks) which has an unbelievably positive effect on my productivity.

Following my youthful visits, my road trips from Arizona, and my adjusting to life in the vicinity of the parks, this period of my life could be considered the fourth major age in my relationship with Disney: The Child, The Tourist, The Local, The Office. During this time, I would usually camp out inside of the Animation Building at Disney California Adventure or find a seat in the now-defunct Innoventions Dream Home. These may not seem like the most peaceful areas in which to write, but somehow it worked for me.

While I was happy in The Office Age of my Disney life, it was becoming increasing clear that a new age was dawning: The Retreat. As I was finishing up this book, my wife and I decided to leave California and move to Springfield, Missouri — a city (and state, for that matter) that neither of us had ever been to before dropping in to see if it was somewhere we'd like to live. The idea to move to Springfield may seem random and, to some degree, it was. I stumbled upon it while searching online to see how much rent was in various parts of the country — as I imagine other Angelenos do when they get they get tired of writing four-figured rent checks. Eventually I found a site that quizzes you about what was important for you to have in a city.

That's when I realized that, while only a few years ago I would have exclusively answered "Disney," now the only thing I needed in the city I lived in was my wife. When we got married, Rebekah was forced to adapt to the life I had already built in Glendale. This meant she had to find a job as close as she could to the apartment I had chosen years ago, she would need to supply health insurance from her job since my work as an extra or a 1099er wouldn't qualify, and accept that we would have to live with a roommate in order to afford our two bedroom apartment.

Shortly before our one-year wedding anniversary, our roommate moved out and, after a couple of attempts to replace her, we decided it was time to be alone. Of course, this meant we would be spending a lot more in rent and so I took on extra hours at the theatre. However, after only a few months, I decided that 12 years at that job was enough and that it was time to think seriously about what I wanted to do with my life. That's when I came up with the idea for this book.

I had been working on the manuscript for a few months before leaving the theatre, but had stopped partially because I wanted to start sending out proposals for the book to various publishers and partially because working at the theatre full time proved too exhausting. Granted, working 40 hours wasn't that hard, but the constant stress and anxiety I felt while there meant I wanted to do nothing more than rest when I got home. It was becoming increasingly clear to me that my job was holding me back from what I really wanted to be doing.

Rebekah was starting to feel about the same way. Not only had her job not turned out to be what she thought it would but they had also started cutting back her hours and changing her role. While she had no problem with living in California, she too was excited by the prospect of something new that neither of us had experienced; a life we could call our own.

During the week of Christmas, Rebekah was off of work due to the holiday and so we had three days in which to drive to Missouri and see what we thought of a place the internet told us we would like. When Bekah got home from work, we packed some small bags and hopped in the car. Taking turns driving every five hours or so, we made it to Springfield without making any extended stops. We checked in to a hotel for the evening and had an appointment to see an apartment the next morning.

After dropping off our bags in the room, we set out to see some of the city and maybe get some dinner. Since we had arrived, it had been pouring — something we certainly hadn't seen in Los Angeles for some time. We drove through the downtown area, but the rain made it hard to see much. Instead, we decided to head to the local mall.

Walking in, the first thing I noticed was that there was a ceiling mere feet above my head as opposed to another level or two of stores as I was used to from frequenting California shopping centers. There was a real sense of, "This is it?" during our entire tour of the place, but we soon realized it had more or less everything we'd need — minus an Apple or Disney Store.

It was clear that, should we pull the trigger, this move would involve a bit of culture shock. Although I was a little disappointed with what I found in the city, I tried to tell myself that I probably didn't give it a fair shake because of the rain. Luckily, this proved true.

The next morning, we arrived at what was to be our new home. We decided to stick with a two bedroom apartment so that we could turn the extra room into an office for me to work in, since Disneyland would no longer be an option. In addition to the lovely lake filled with adorable ducks, the cozy community room that hosted monthly socials, and the pool and hot tub that were offered year round (not that you'd want to use them year round), our rent including internet and cable was to be less than half of what we were paying in Glendale.

We started our move a month later, hitting the road the day after my birthday. It's funny to think that my wife and I, who were born just 18 days apart, would be celebrating our birthdays in two different states, but that's how it happened. By the time her's came around, we were pretty much settled in and I got to work finishing my book.

Part of the deal we made to each other when we moved here was that my wife and I would use some of the money we're saving to see more of the world. This of course means first time trips to Hong Kong Disneyland, Disneyland Paris, and the soon to be opened Shanghai Disneyland in addition to return trips to Disneyland, Walt Disney World, and Tokyo Disneyland. Perhaps this will mean a sixth age for me? The World Traveler?

As Disneyland turns 60 this year, there's been a lot of reflection on just how much has changed over the past six decades since Walt introduced us to his dream. On a much smaller scale, writing this book has lead me to think about how much I've personally changed and grown over nearly half that time. Reliving it now has reminded me again that I truly have had an E-Ticket life so far... and it's far from over.

Bonus Material
"The E-Ticket Life" Blog Entries

In October of 2014 (on my one-year wedding anniversary), I launched a blog on LaughingPlace.com under the name "The E-Ticket Life." This, of course, is no coincidence as it was always the intent that the blog and the eventual book (the one you're reading now) would share a storytelling style and perspective. However, since the blog was weekly, with a new entry being posted every Saturday, the stories and essays of the blog quickly became somehow related to the events of the previous week… no matter how loosely.

Because of the nature of the blog — the weekly deadline, the topical restraints, and, again, the weekly deadline — "The E-Ticket Life" blog is often sillier, leaner, and smaller in scope than the entries of the book. Still, I feel the audience that Laughing Place and I have grown through the blog reflects what I've believed the whole time while writing this book: Disney fans have an appetite for this type of storytelling and essay writing.

As an added bonus, I've included three of what are not only my favorite entries from the first six months of the blog but also those that our readers voted on as their favorites. Thankfully, these entries are also three that don't rely heavily on the images and videos that I'm keen to include on my digital platform. I hope you enjoy these blog entries for what they are and I hope you'll join us every Saturday on LaughingPlace.com for another journey into "The E-Ticket Life" blog.

October 11, 2014
Candy Corn Acres

Back before Buena Vista Street there was Sunshine Plaza. And every year for Halloween the plaza would become Candy Corn Acres — a farm that would produce oversized candy corns, but lacked any actual treats for consumption. Yes it was tacky and random but I liked it. My affinity for it probably spurs less from the display itself and more from that time in my life I associate it with.

Circa 2008 I had just moved back into my dad's house and found myself with a lot of free time. Instead of doing something productive to ensure that I could stop living in my dad's house I choose to waste time on the internet watching YouTube and listening to a new form of media called "podcasts." Back then, the shows I listened to were mainly actual radio shows that chopped their broadcasts into segments to posted online. As a result, I was completely ignorant to the blossoming world that was growing right under me.

One evening, I wondered to myself if there were any Disney-centric podcasts and ran a search not expecting many results, if any. To my surprise, I found several. The first podcasts I downloaded were *The Laughing Place Podcast* and Aaron Wallace's *Zip-A-Dee-Doo-Pod*. Both of these were great but, as a nearly-west-coaster, I was interested in finding a show that covered Disneyland. That's when I stumbled upon *Disneyland News Today*, hosted by a little British kid named Luke Manning. At the time, I actually didn't realize how young Luke was — 14 or so at the time — but started to pick up on clues throughout the months that I listened.

I was instantly hooked on these shows and was soon consuming far more Disney news and info than I ever thought possible. Listening to these shows also increased my impulse to head back out to Disneyland and soon I was sneaking my way out there once every other month or so.

A few trips in, I decided I wanted to try my hand at podcasting and running my own Disney-fan site. I racked my brain for a URL that was Disney enough without being too overt (for the record, I've always thought that "Laughing Place" was brilliant for that reason). The name I eventually settled on was "Somewhere in Particular," which was supposed to be a reference to Mr. Toad's trip to nowhere in particular. I justified this with the fact that Mr. Toad was now a Disneyland exclusive ride and that the show and site would be about somewhere in particular: Disneyland. If that wasn't bad enough, I branded my Twitter to go along with my new site name and became @SIParticular — a name that no one knew how to pronounce leading many to just refer to me as "sip." In hindsight (and even at the time), I realized this was a pretty terrible name. Still, I was so anxious to get everything up that I didn't care.

All of the Disney sites I followed included photo report updates of what was new in the parks. Thus, for my next Disney trip, I made sure to get a new digital camera (or, as we call them now, "cameras") in order to document all the new sights I encountered on my visit. As luck would have it, I arrived just days before Halloween Time at the Disneyland resort began. This was back when DCA actually hosted the Disneyland Halloween parties and much of the festive theming (aside from Haunted Mansion Holiday) occupied that park.

When I arrived at Disney's California Adventure (yes, it still had the apostrophe 's' back then), I was overly excited to see that the Candy Corn Acres displays had already been installed. I walked towards them wide eyed as I reached for my camera and proceed to snap shots of every detail. I also waited patiently to get the perfect shot of Heimlich as he popped out of the giant candy corn near the plaza's fountain.

At the time, I felt like I had gotten a real scoop. I even confirmed with a Cast Member that this was indeed the first day the displays had been open. Of course, what I had forgotten was that, if no one follows you, it's nearly impossible to break news. Not to mention that this wasn't the first year Candy Corn Acres had existed and thus the level of excitement anyone had for it dissipated quickly.

Regardless, I spent hours uploading, editing and categorizing my hundreds of photos when I got home and immediately posted them to my site. I think it might have been one of maybe three photo reports that went up on Somewhere in Particular before I abandoned the project. I also got one episode in before I realized that the reason I wanted to have a podcast wasn't just to talk to myself about Disney but to engage others in conversation about it — something that was sorely missing in my show's original (and only) incarnation.

A few months later, I declined to renew my domain name, changed my Twitter handle to my real moniker, and went back to just being a podcast listener until I joined *The Disneyland Gazette* in 2010. By then, DCA was under heavy construction and Candy Corn Acres was a thing of the past.

As I said, Candy Corn Acres wasn't great. In fact, you could probably argue that it was another example of what was wrong with DCA 1.0 with its half-baked attempts to court guests. But, like DCA, I too had to realize that what I was doing wasn't working. For one, I had spent money on a camera and trips to California instead of saving up to move out of my parent's house at the age of 22. Secondly, instead of taking the time to flesh-out my ideas and bring others on board, I was too hasty and proud to think that I would fail. What seemed like a great idea at the time might have brought a few smiles, but ultimately needed retooling.

The next year, I not only moved out of my dad's house but also moved to California. I even got the company I worked for to pay for me to move and I situated myself equal distance from work and Disneyland — a much more reasonable solution than driving out from Arizona once a month. Since then, I've felt transformed but that doesn't mean I still don't get nostalgic about those lazy and misguided days, if not only to remind myself how much I've grown.

So RIP Candy Corn Acres, Somewhere in Particular and Kyle Burbank 1.0.

November 29, 2014
The Pros and Cons of a Phenomenon

This past week, America celebrated Thanksgiving, where many count their blessings by over-eating. Then there's Black Friday, where we lose our minds to take advantage of the hot deals. Both days could be described as "too much of a good thing," which is why it seems perfect to me that *Frozen* also celebrated its one year anniversary this week.

Like many I know, I was trepidatious when it came to *Frozen*. When my friend and I first saw the teaser attached to *Monsters University*, we remarked that it looked less like the classic Disney princess tales and more like *Ice Age*. Instead, the film was everything you could have wanted and the box office totals reflected this.

I remember reading Box Office Mojo a few days before the film's release (as I regularly do) and saw them say of *Frozen*, "It's tough to imagine it matching *Tangled*'s $68.7 million." Oops. *Frozen* actually made almost as much over the three-day weekend as *Tangled* made in five and ended up taking in over $93 million by the end of the holiday weekend. By the end of its run, *Frozen* doubled *Tangled* box office total, making just over $400 million.

By that time, lines to meet Anna and Elsa were reaching insane levels on both coasts, the character's dresses were selling out as soon as they hit the racks, and rumors were swirling not only about a sequel to the film but also a Broadway stage production. This was also about the time people began to speculate on how *Frozen* would make its way into the parks. Actually, not just "how" but "how soon?"

The first major announcement aside from the meet and greet shuffling at Walt Disney World was the introduction of *Frozen Summer Fun LIVE!* at Disney Hollywood Studios. This promotion included a parade, stage show, play area, merchandising, and a fireworks spectacular. This is all fine and good since 1) DHS is themed to movies so really anything is fair game and 2) DHS is also going through an identity crisis and could use some attractions to distract from all the others they are shuttering. Of course, the festivities were extended beyond the titular summer and, though the offerings have been downscaled, the stage show and merchandising continued.

Frozen's offerings in Hollywood Studios were partially viewed as a way to keep guests in Walt Disney World and away from the recently opened Diagon Alley expansion of The Wizarding World of Harry Potter over in Universal. Just like in that series' third film, *The Prisoner of Azkaban*, this is when I began to sing to myself, "Something wicked this way comes."

It's interesting to think about how "New Fantasyland" would have turned out if they had just waited a couple of extra years until *Frozen* had hit. Would there be a *Little Mermaid* ride there today? Or would it have been the Mine Train to get the ax? Unfortunately for Disney, the literally just completed Fantasyland expansion (apparently) left no room for their rising stars. So, instead, they turned their sights to Epcot and, after months of every Disney fan knowing what they were going to decide, they pulled the trigger on their questionable plan.

Whatever you think of the Maelstrom or *Frozen*, hear me out on my view of the whole matter. Epcot has always been a place of edu-tainment, and I believe keeping this spirit alive is in Disney's best interest. Through the years, World Showcase has been successful in integrating characters in spite of the fact that they were initially banned when the park opened. To me, their inclusion doesn't just make the park more tourist friendly but also serves as a point of entry for children and adults to learn about the real country and culture that the characters come from. Even when they added The Three Caballeros to the Mexico Pavillon ride, the attraction still sought to show the beautiful sites and exciting culture of our neighbors to the south.

This is why I had no problem with Anna and Elsa doing meet and greets in Norway. Sure Arendelle wasn't Norway, but the inspiration the country had on the fictional version was enough to make this a win for the Norwegian Chamber of Commerce. Having young girls meet the popular princesses (well, one princess and one queen) and then learning about another culture sounds exactly like Epcot edu-tainment to me.

On the other hand, turning the Maelstrom into a *Frozen* attraction, as it has been argued by of my friend, does a disservice to both the Norway Pavillon as well as *Frozen*. Obviously we have no idea what this attraction will be exactly, but it stands to reason that it won't be the cast of the film teaching you about Norwegian folklore and this is a shame. By turning Norway into Arendelle, Disney is compromising the integrity of World Showcase and its purpose. I recently joked that I really want *Big Hero 6* to do well, but I also would like to keep Japan as Japan and not San Fransokyo.

My argument isn't even really about Maelstrom itself. I've never been on Stitch's Great Escape and I will never go on it as long as I can help it. However, if Disney wanted to replace it with a *Frozen* attraction, I'd strongly object since *Frozen* has no business in Tomorrowland — a land that already has some thematic issues. Like I said, I'm more concerned about the overall impact this will have on Epcot and World Showcase going forward. Of course, I'll have to reserve my final judgement until the attraction opens.

When the Maelstrom controversy exploded, there were many who saw no problem with it and saw the detractors as hating on *Frozen*. Trust me, I love *Frozen*. I saw it multiple times in theatres, met Anna and Elsa, and, while on my trip to Tokyo earlier this year, I made a point to pick up both the Japanese and Korean versions of the soundtrack. To avoid annoying Twitter fights, I never said this but I always thought, "Just wait until *Frozen* takes away something you love."

That foreshadowing phrase came to fruition recently as Disney announced that the Mad T Party in Disney California Adventure (which, for some reason, attracted large weekly crowds) would be coming to an end. They never said that *Frozen* attractions akin to the DHS promotion were coming, but please. Presumably this plan may have also lead to the death of DCA's Muppet*Vision 3D, which closed "temporarily" without much notice or many noticing.

When Carsland was built, my friend Aaron Wallace made a point that really stuck with me. He said that if Walt Disney thought the way Bob Iger did, Frontierland would have been called Davy Crockett Land. The point being that the Disney of late loves to pounce on the "new hotness" — to borrow a phrase from Will Smith — at the expense of evergreen theming.

On Thanksgiving, did you finish that last mound of mashed potatoes and then sit back wondering if that might have been too much too fast? How long until Disney does that with *Frozen?*

Editor's note: At the time this book is being published, Mad T Party has actually returned to Disney California Adventure but For the First Time in Forever still occupies the Muppet*Vision Theatre.

January 10, 2015
Hello, McFly

If you're not a huge *Back to the Future* buff, surely the endless articles comparing the 2015 of the film series' second entry to the real thing have tipped you off to this 30 year milestone. To celebrate our arrival into the future, The Egyptian theatre in Hollywood (just a few blocks from Disney's El Capitan) offered a triple feature last weekend that I attended with my friend Josh. I hadn't seen the films properly since I was maybe 10 years old and I was surprised how perfect the original flick was. Both sequels were good as well (I'm partial to part two since I'm not a huge fan of Westerns), making this one of the best film series of all time.

Unlike many patrons, I choose not to dress as any character from the film to attend my screenings, mainly because I don't own any puffy vests. Instead, I — being the theme park geek that I am — wore my Krustyland crew jacket since that attraction replaced the BTTF rides in Hollywood and Orlando. In said ride, guests start in the distant future (2015) chasing film antagonist Biff Tannen, who has taken hold of Doc Brown's flying

DeLorean time machine. From there, you head into the ice age and then prehistoric times for run-ins with dinosaurs and volcanic explosions. All the while, riders are experiencing simulated flight, falls, and presumably a spray of water at some point. In other words, it was like every other Universal Studios attraction ever built.

As you can probably guess, aside from a few small coincidences, the film and ride didn't get much right about our current year. What's interesting is that the film's starting point (and original release date) of 1985 was imagined to be far more advanced than it turned out be — at least according to Walt Disney.

From the start, Tommorland was a troublesome theme for a land given the speed of innovation (sidenote: can you believe the first iPhone came out eight years ago?!). Originally, the Tomorrow of Tomorrowland was 1986, which just so happens to be the year I was born and one year after *Back to the Future*'s release. In the first few years, the land added a couple of interesting views of what technology would soon look like in the form of the often joked about Bathroom of Tomorrow and The House of the Future.

Other than Imagineers correctly guessing that Monsanto would come to rule our lives in the next century, The House of the Future now seems as laughable as *Back to the Future*'s 2015 does. It's not that a lot of these ideas aren't doable (though, to my knowledge, the flying car is still a ways off), but perhaps it's just that no one really feels the need to have a bushel of grapes descend from their kitchen ceiling — an idea I'm pretty sure they stole from the Tiki Room.

Today, Tomorrowland functions less as a land about what the actual future will look like and more on science fiction (including one property that actually takes place "a long long time ago" if its opening scroll is to be believed) and anything related to outer space. Though you'd probably be hard pressed to find a self-respecting Disney fan who doesn't think that two o'clock quadrant of the Magic Kingdom and Disneyland wasn't in need of some overhauling, I'd still say that Tomorrowland is my favorite of the lands thanks to its kinetic energy and nostalgic optimism — i. e. "There's a great, big, beautiful tomorrow."

It seems to me that "Tomorrowland" is no longer a conjunction of two words but its own, unique, one-word theme; a theme that encompasses a different kind of imagination than its neighboring Fantasyland. Where as the land of Fantasy dreams of personal achievements, Tomorrowland dreams of innovations that will better humanity… or just burp chili dog in your face. Sure there are still questions as to where exactly a portal to Monstropolis or a "race" in an infuriatingly slow vehicle fit in to all this, but just humor me for a moment.

In *Back to the Future Part II*, Marty and Doc enter an alternate 1985 where Biff has become a powerful multimillionaire. While that's a grim version, there's also the happier '85 shown at the end of the original film featuring the improved lives the McFly's enjoyed since George learned to stand up for himself. I'd like to think that the Tomorrowlands we have are more like an alternate timeline that incorporate different versions of the past, present, and that third one. It's impossible to guess the future correctly without looking like a fool when it doesn't come true. But Tomorrowland can't get the future wrong if it just stops guessing.

Acknowledgements

Of all the things I thought I'd accomplish in my life, writing a book was not one of them. Needless to say there are many people without whom this would not have been possible and deserve to be acknowledged.

First I'd like to thank my amazing wife Rebekah who supported and inspired me throughout the entire process. Also, you would not be reading this right now if not for Benji Breitbart and Doobie Moseley of Laughing Place. Both gentlemen believed in me and this project enough to help me see it through to this point. For that, I am eternally grateful.

My vision for this book would not have been fully realized without additions from two talented individuals: Aaron Wallace and Ashley O'Neill. I am humbled and honored to share the credit for this project with both them.

From the moment I conceived the idea for this book, I knew I wanted Aaron to write the foreword not only because of his experience writing *The Thinking Fan's Guide to Walt Disney World* but because of the expertise and thoughtfulness he would bring. Not only did he deliver in spades, but he was always willing to lend an ear to my questions and offer his advice. He also introduced me to my wife, so shout out for that.

Similarly, when I presented Ashley with my plans for the book, I knew she would knock it out of the park. Sometimes her illustrations would bring to life exactly what I had envisioned and other times she surprised me by coming up with something more brilliant than I ever could have dreamed. Her work truly brings another level of emotion to this book that I so desired and I thank her for it.

I'd like to thank my family: Ken & Missy Burbank, Robyn Burbank, Alma Bagby, and Scott Burbank.

The past and present staff of The Disneyland Gazette: Luke Manning, Kenny Siegel, Connie Moreno, Myrna Litt, David Spencer, Daniel Hale, Mallory Fosket, Chuck and Leigh Canzoneri, Shawn Hutchison, and Kim Schroeder.

My *Star Wars and Starbucks* co-hosts: Josh Sussman and Chris Bergoch

Everyone else at Laughing Place: Rebekah Moseley, Alex Reif, Roger Rodriguez, and Doug Marsh.

I'd also like to thank the HUGE list of people who directly or indirectly contributed to this book including (in alphabetical order):

Toren Ajk	Stacie Hale	Arielle Nadel
Robert Allison	Brandon Hawkins	Heather Mutter
Steven Amiri	Jordan Christian Hearn	Emily Nadolski
Marisa Baram	Robert Heaston	Heather Palmer
Brian &	Sarah Hungerford	Alexis Pascarella
Monica Bauer	Brian Indrelunas	Mike Passine
Becca Blumenfeld	Joey Inigo	Dominic Passine
Thomas Boyd	Miranda Rae Jensen	Missy Patterson
Cara-Lynn Branch	Alyssa Jones	Michael Peterson
Kyle Burch	Susan Kellogg	Jaimee Piccolo
Elizabeth Caldwell	Mic Knight	Kristin Piccolo
Joseph Casabona	April Rose Krack	Andrew Rezende
Raymond Castro	Ashley LaRue	Kevin Ronan
Steven Causey	Joyce Lasley	Jamie Ruiz
Stephen &	Todd LeComte	Christina Sanchez
Libby Champion	Vanessa Lengies	Amir Sarooghi
Leila Cole Ciszewski	David Lepore	Nick Smith
Shellace Star Deavila	Janet Lopez	Danielle Thompson
Jeff DePaoli	Jesse Magee	Roger Udwin
Patrick Dougall	Kyle McCormick	Kristen Ursenbach
Travis Dwyer	Caitlin McGarry	Martina Vondrick
Adam &	Nate Meads	Adrienne Wade
Cassandra Ehrig	Desiree Medina	Jeff Wang &
Grainne Evans	Ryan Middledorf	Heather Wagner
Charlotte Evaraert	Chuck &	Jill Whitfield
Lucia Fascano	Diane Mlinarcik	Stephanie Wilcox
Shelby Fry	Stephen Mlinarcik &	Jay Williams
Jim Fuller	Concetta Morabito	Laura Wolak
Edrina Bliss Gibson	Matthew &	Alex Wolff
Alexis Gonzalez	Kahri Mlinarcik	Brianna Young
Reuben Gutierrez	Chloe Mlinarcik	
Justin Guzman	Leah Mlinarcik	..and anyone I
Wendi Hale	Sara Moran	regrettably forgot

Finally I'd like to thank all of the readers, some of which I just happen to know by name:

Jason Lindley, Jacquie Nahom, Sophie and Sarah Siegel,
The Mannings, Marshall Blankenship, Brittney Maranville,
Jeff Peterson, Sharon Kamprath, Cheryl Buchanan,
Darren Walsh, Carol P. Crum, Jeff Bronk,
Jonathan de Caussin, Zoe and Haley Bales, Lori Hungerford,
Travis Garrett, Jon Katayanagi, Jennifer Dutrow,
Jennifer A. Farmer, Linda Holtorf, Steven Schwarzrock,
Keefe Chow, Justin Smith, Dave Peloso,
and the good folks at DizneyCoastToCoast.com.

THANK YOU!

About the Artist

Ashley O'Neill has spent the majority of her life in Southern California where she and her mother had season passes to Disneyland in her youth. This lead to being pulled out of class early to play hooky nearly once a week. Being a straight 'A' student, Ashley wasn't too worried about flunking... and if she did, it would be justified.

She showed an affinity for sketching at a young age, even winning an award in the Los Angeles State Fair. But, much to her own disappointment in later years, didn't take direction well from art instructors. Thus she took to theater to express her imagination and water polo to work off those pesky "brooding artist" tendencies.

Immediately following her graduation, Ashley attended Cal Poly Pomona intending to earn a Bachelors in biology — fearing for the financial burden an art degree may lead to. Unfortunately, she failed to remember her ineptitude for mathematics. She swiftly switched to a degree in history where she specialized in the ancient Near East. All the while, she continued her high school job at the movie theater where she met Kyle Burbank and worked as his fellow manager.

While she remains bound to management for the company she's been with since the age of 17, she has a lucrative business designing tattoos and drawing for those who have last-minute school art projects and cash to spare. Preferring to work with traditional mediums, such as pencil, ink and markers, Ashley tends to create all her work by hand. This is the first of her major accomplishments and is very grateful for the experience.

About the Author

Kyle Burbank is a freelance writer living in Springfield, Missouri. Previously, he lived in Glendale, California and spent years working on some of the biggest sets in Hollywood... as an extra.

Prior to moving to Los Angeles, Kyle grew up in Chandler, Arizona and graduated from Chandler High School in 2004. While still in high school, he wrote for the school's student newspaper, *The Wolf Howl*. It was in those articles that Kyle established his voice as a writer, humorist, and commentator.

After moving to California in 2009, Kyle's passion for Disney worked its way into his career. After briefly starting his own Disney-fan podcast, he came aboard to start *The Disneyland Gazette* in 2010. Five years later, the podcast has produced over 200 episodes. Additionally, he has also been a guest on *Zip-a-Dee-Doo-Pod, The Hub Podcast, Dizney Coast to Coast,* and *Behind the Magic.*

In October of 2013, Kyle married Rebekah Mlinarcik in a small service. Later that year, he joined the writing staff at LaughingPlace.com — one of the oldest and largest Disney fan sites on the web. In addition to serving as one of the site's Los Angeles correspondents, he launched "The E-Ticket Life" as a weekly blog in October of 2014.

Over the years, Kyle has written several speculative screenplays and teleplays. He also wrote, directed, and starred in the short film *Blythe. The E-Ticket Life: Stories, Essays, and Lessons Learned from My Decidedly Disney Travels* is his first book.

Kyle can be found online at KyleBurbank.com

Made in the USA
Middletown, DE
18 August 2015